EXPLORING THE WORLD OF DATA SCIENCE AND MACHINE LEARNING

UNLEASHING THE POWER OF DATA-DRIVEN INSIGHTS AND INTELLIGENT ALGORITHMS

WRITTEN BY NIBEDITA SAHU

Table of Contents

Title: Exploring the World of Data Science and Machine Learning

Author: Nibedita Sahu

Preface:

Welcome to "Exploring the World of Data Science and Machine Learning." This book is designed to provide a holistic understanding of data science and machine learning concepts, from the fundamentals to advanced techniques. Whether you're a student, professional, or an individual curious about the field, this book will equip you with the knowledge and skills necessary to excel in this rapidly evolving domain.

Instructions:

Before delving into the chapters, it is essential to understand the basics of data science and machine learning. Familiarize yourself with Python programming, as it will be the primary language used throughout the book. Additionally, grasp the foundational concepts of statistics, as they form the backbone of data analysis and modeling.

Take your time to absorb the content, as each chapter builds upon the previous ones.

Make use of the practical examples and exercises provided to solidify your understanding.

Don't hesitate to explore additional resources and online communities to deepen your knowledge.

Stay curious and keep practicing, as data science and machine learning require continuous learning and application.

Now, let's begin our journey through the captivating world of data science and machine learning!

Book Description:

"Exploring the World of Data Science and Machine Learning" is a comprehensive guide for individuals interested in delving into the fascinating fields of data science and machine learning. Written by Nibedita Sahu, a passionate data science and machine learning enthusiast, this book provides a practical and beginner-friendly approach to understanding the core concepts, techniques, and applications of these rapidly evolving fields.

Author Description:

Nibedita Sahu is a dedicated data science and machine learning enthusiast with a profound interest in leveraging data-driven insights to solve complex problems. With a background in mathematics and expertise in Python programming, Nibedita is well-versed in the fundamental concepts and tools of data science. As a tech blogger, author, article writer, content creator, and graphic designer, she enjoys sharing her knowledge and experiences with a wider audience, making complex concepts accessible to beginners.

Table of Contents:

Outlines:

Chapter 1: Introduction to Data Science and Machine Learning

In this chapter, we will explore the fundamental concepts of data science and machine learning. We will discuss the importance of data and the role of data scientists in extracting valuable insights. Furthermore, we will differentiate between supervised and unsupervised learning and outline the process of building machine learning models.

Chapter 2: Foundations of Statistics

To embark on a data science journey, it is crucial to understand the basics of statistics. This chapter will cover essential statistical concepts such as probability, hypothesis testing, and statistical distributions. We will also delve into descriptive and inferential statistics and their applications in data analysis.

Chapter 3: Python for Data Science

Python is a powerful programming language extensively used in data science and machine learning. In this chapter, we will familiarize ourselves with Python's syntax, data structures, and libraries commonly employed in data science projects. We will learn to manipulate data, perform computations, and visualize results using libraries such as NumPy, Pandas, and Matplotlib.

Chapter 4: Data Wrangling and Cleaning

Data is rarely clean and ready for analysis. This chapter will guide you through the process of data wrangling and cleaning. We will learn how to handle missing data, handle outliers, and transform variables for better model performance. Techniques such as data imputation, outlier detection, and feature scaling will be explored.

Chapter 5: Exploratory Data Analysis

Before diving into modeling, it is crucial to gain insights from the data through exploratory data analysis (EDA). This chapter will introduce various techniques to explore and visualize data effectively.

We will examine data distributions, relationships between variables, and identify patterns and outliers that can inform our modeling decisions.

Chapter 6: Supervised Learning: Regression

Regression analysis is a powerful technique for predicting numerical outcomes. In this chapter, we will delve into supervised learning algorithms for regression tasks. We will explore linear regression, decision tree regression, and other regression models. We will learn how to train models, evaluate their performance, and interpret the results.

Chapter 7: Supervised Learning: Classification

Classification is the process of assigning data points to predefined classes or categories. In this chapter, we will explore supervised learning algorithms for classification tasks. We will delve into logistic regression, support vector machines, decision trees, and ensemble methods such as random forests. We will learn about model evaluation metrics and techniques to handle imbalanced datasets.

Chapter 8: Unsupervised Learning: Clustering

Unsupervised learning allows us to discover patterns and structures within unlabeled data. This chapter will focus on clustering algorithms, including k-means clustering, hierarchical clustering, and DBSCAN. We will learn how to identify groups or clusters in the data and interpret the results.

Chapter 9: Dimensionality Reduction

High-dimensional data can be challenging to visualize and model. Dimensionality reduction techniques help us represent data in a lower-dimensional space without losing essential information. In this chapter, we will explore principal component analysis (PCA), t-SNE, and other dimensionality reduction methods.

Chapter 10: Feature Engineering and Selection

Feature engineering involves creating new features from existing data to improve model performance. In this chapter, we will discuss techniques such as feature scaling, one-hot encoding, and feature extraction. Additionally, we will learn about feature selection methods to identify the most relevant features for modeling.

Chapter 11: Model Evaluation and Validation

Evaluating model performance and validating the models are critical steps in the machine learning pipeline. This chapter will introduce evaluation metrics such as accuracy, precision, recall, and F1-score. We will also explore techniques like cross-validation, hyperparameter tuning, and model selection to ensure robust and reliable models.

Chapter 12: Ensemble Methods

Ensemble methods combine multiple models to improve predictive performance. In this chapter, we will explore ensemble techniques such as bagging, boosting, and stacking. We will understand how ensemble methods work and how to implement them using popular libraries such as scikit-learn.

Chapter 13: Deep Learning and Neural Networks

Deep learning has revolutionized the field of machine learning, particularly in domains such as computer vision and natural language processing. This chapter will introduce neural networks, deep learning architectures, and popular frameworks like TensorFlow and Keras. We will explore convolutional neural networks (CNNs), recurrent neural networks (RNNs), and deep learning applications.

Chapter 14: Natural Language Processing

Natural Language Processing (NLP) enables machines to understand and interpret human language. In this chapter, we will dive into NLP techniques such as text preprocessing, sentiment analysis, and text classification. We will also explore language models like Word2Vec and transformer models like BERT.

Chapter 15: Time Series Analysis

Time series data is prevalent in various domains, including finance, weather forecasting, and stock market analysis. This chapter will cover time series analysis techniques, including data decomposition, trend analysis, and forecasting models such as ARIMA and LSTM.

Chapter 16: Recommender Systems

Recommender systems have become an integral part of modern online platforms. In this chapter, we will explore collaborative filtering and content-based recommender systems. We will learn how to build recommendation engines that provide personalized recommendations to users.

Chapter 17: Anomaly Detection

Anomaly detection involves identifying unusual patterns or outliers in data. This chapter will introduce techniques like statistical methods, clustering-based approaches, and machine learning-based approaches for anomaly detection. We will discuss real-world applications and challenges in detecting anomalies.

Chapter 18: Deploying Machine Learning Models

Deploying machine learning models into production requires considerations beyond modeling. This chapter will cover topics such as model deployment, model serving, and scalability. We will explore frameworks like Flask and Django to create APIs for model deployment.

Chapter 19: Ethical Considerations in Data Science

As data scientists, we have a responsibility to consider the ethical implications of our work. This chapter will discuss ethical considerations in data science, including privacy, bias, and fairness. We will explore techniques to address bias and ensure fairness in machine learning models.

Chapter 20: Future Trends and Advances in Data Science and Machine Learning

Data science and machine learning are constantly evolving fields. In this final chapter, we will explore emerging trends such as explainable AI, federated learning, and automated machine learning (AutoML).

We will discuss how these advancements are shaping the future of data science and machine learning.

Appendix: Resources and References

This appendix provides a curated list of resources, including books, online courses, and research papers, to further explore the topics covered in this book. Additionally, it includes references and citations for the various concepts and techniques discussed throughout the chapters.

Congratulations! We have completed the initial outline for the book "Exploring the World of Data Science and Machine Learning."

Chapter 1: Introduction to Data Science and Machine Learning

1.1 Overview

In recent years, the fields of data science and machine learning have gained significant attention and have become integral components of various industries. With the advent of big data and advancements in computing power, businesses and organizations are now able to leverage the power of data to gain valuable insights and make informed decisions. This chapter serves as an introduction to the fundamental concepts of data science and machine learning, highlighting their importance and providing an overview of the processes involved in building machine learning models.

1.2 The Importance of Data

Data is the foundation of data science and machine learning. It is the raw material that allows us to gain insights, identify patterns, and make predictions. The availability and accessibility of vast amounts of data have revolutionized the way we approach problem-solving and decision-making. By analyzing data, organizations can uncover hidden trends, understand customer behavior, optimize business processes, and improve overall performance.

Data comes in various forms, such as structured, unstructured, and semi-structured data. Structured data is highly organized and follows a predefined format, often found in relational databases. Unstructured data, on the other hand, lacks a specific structure and includes text, images, audio, and video files. Semi-structured data falls somewhere in between, with some organization but also flexibility in its structure. By leveraging different types of data, data scientists can gain a comprehensive understanding of complex systems and phenomena.

1.3 The Role of Data Scientists

Data scientists play a crucial role in extracting valuable insights from data. They are skilled professionals who possess a combination of expertise in statistics, programming, and domain knowledge. Data scientists are responsible for collecting and cleaning data, performing exploratory data analysis, developing and implementing machine learning models, and interpreting the results.

One of the primary tasks of a data scientist is to transform raw data into a usable format. This process, known as data preprocessing, involves cleaning the data by removing inconsistencies, handling missing values, and dealing with outliers. Data scientists also need to perform exploratory data analysis (EDA) to understand the underlying patterns, relationships, and distributions within the data. EDA techniques include visualizations, statistical summaries, and data profiling.

Once the data is preprocessed and analyzed, data scientists can develop machine learning models to extract insights and make predictions. Machine learning is a subset of artificial intelligence (AI) that enables computers to learn from data and improve their performance on a specific task over time. It is divided into two main categories: supervised learning and unsupervised learning.

1.4 Supervised Learning

Supervised learning is a type of machine learning where the model learns from labeled examples. In supervised learning, the dataset consists of input features (also known as predictors or independent variables) and corresponding output labels (also known as target variables or dependent variables). The goal is to learn a mapping function that can predict the output labels for new, unseen inputs accurately.

There are different types of supervised learning algorithms, including regression and classification. Regression models are used when the output labels are continuous or numerical values, such as predicting the price of a house based on its features. Classification models, on the other hand, are used when the output labels belong to a discrete set of classes, such as classifying emails as spam or non-spam.

To build a supervised learning model, data scientists typically split the available data into two subsets: a training set and a testing set. The training set is used to train the model, while the testing set is used to evaluate its performance. Evaluation metrics such as accuracy, precision, recall, and F1 score are used to assess the model's performance.

1.5 Unsupervised Learning

Unlike supervised learning, unsupervised learning does not involve labeled data. In unsupervised learning, the goal is to discover hidden patterns, structures, or relationships in the data without any prior knowledge or guidance. Unsupervised learning algorithms explore the data and identify inherent clusters, associations, or anomalies.

Clustering is a common unsupervised learning technique used to group similar data points together. It helps identify patterns and segment the data into meaningful subsets. Another technique is dimensionality reduction, which aims to reduce the number of input features while preserving important information. This is particularly useful for visualizing high-dimensional data and reducing computational complexity.

Unsupervised learning algorithms are valuable for exploratory data analysis and can provide insights into the underlying structure of the data. They can also be used as a preprocessing step for supervised learning tasks, such as identifying relevant features or reducing noise in the data.

1.6 Building Machine Learning Models

The process of building machine learning models involves several steps, including data collection, preprocessing, feature engineering, model selection, model training, model evaluation, and deployment.

Data collection is the first step, where data scientists gather relevant data from various sources. This can include structured data from databases, unstructured data from text documents, or external data from APIs or web scraping.

Once the data is collected, it needs to be preprocessed to ensure its quality and usability. This involves handling missing values, encoding categorical variables, scaling numerical features, and splitting the data into training and testing sets.

Feature engineering is the process of transforming raw data into meaningful features that can be used by machine learning algorithms. This can involve creating new features, selecting relevant features, or transforming existing features to improve the model's performance.

Model selection is an essential step in building machine learning models. There are various algorithms available, each with its strengths and weaknesses. The choice of algorithm depends on the problem at hand, the type of data, and the desired outcome. It is crucial to select the most appropriate algorithm to achieve accurate and reliable predictions.

Once the model is selected, it needs to be trained on the training data. Training involves finding the optimal parameters or coefficients that minimize the difference between the predicted and actual values. This is done using optimization algorithms, such as gradient descent or stochastic gradient descent.

After training, the model's performance needs to be evaluated on the testing data. Evaluation metrics, such as accuracy, precision, recall, and F1 score, are used to assess the model's predictive power. If the model performs well, it can be deployed in a real-world setting to make predictions on new, unseen data.

1.7 The Challenges of Data Science and Machine Learning

While data science and machine learning offer tremendous opportunities, they also come with various challenges. It's important to be aware of these challenges and address them appropriately to ensure accurate and reliable results.

1.7.1 Data Quality and Preprocessing

Data quality is a critical factor in the success of any data science or machine learning project. Poor-quality data can lead to biased or incorrect results, making it essential to invest time and effort in data preprocessing. This includes handling missing values, dealing with outliers, addressing data inconsistencies, and ensuring data integrity. Data preprocessing techniques can significantly impact the performance of machine learning models, and careful attention must be given to this step.

1.7.2 Feature Selection and Engineering

Feature selection and engineering involve determining which variables or features are relevant to the problem at hand and transforming them into a suitable format for machine learning algorithms. Choosing the right set of features is crucial for model accuracy and interpretability. However, in high-dimensional datasets, feature selection becomes challenging, and selecting too many or irrelevant features can lead to overfitting. Domain knowledge and exploratory data analysis play a vital role in feature engineering, as they help identify informative features that capture the essence of the problem.

1.7.3 Model Selection and Evaluation

Selecting the appropriate machine learning algorithm for a given problem is not a straightforward task. There are numerous algorithms available, each with its strengths and limitations. The choice of algorithm depends on factors such as the nature of the data, the type of problem (regression, classification, clustering, etc.), and computational requirements. It is crucial to understand the assumptions, limitations, and performance characteristics of different algorithms to make an informed decision. Model evaluation is equally important, as it provides insights into the model's performance and guides further improvements. Care must be taken to choose appropriate evaluation metrics that align with the problem and business objectives.

1.7.4 Overfitting and Underfitting

Overfitting and underfitting are common challenges in machine learning. Overfitting occurs when a model learns the training data too well, resulting in poor generalization to unseen data. It happens when the model is overly complex or when the training data is insufficient. Underfitting, on the other hand, occurs when the model fails to capture the underlying patterns in the data and performs poorly both on the training and testing data. Balancing the complexity of the model, collecting sufficient and diverse training data, and applying regularization techniques can help mitigate these issues.

1.7.5 Ethical Considerations and Bias

Data science and machine learning models are not immune to biases present in the data or the algorithms themselves. Biases can arise due to skewed or incomplete data, algorithmic biases, or biased labeling. It is essential to be aware of these biases and take appropriate measures to mitigate them. This includes performing bias audits, diversifying the training data, and using fairness-aware algorithms. Ethical considerations, such as privacy, data security, and transparency, should also be taken into account throughout the entire data science and machine learning process.

1.8 The Future of Data Science and Machine Learning

As technology continues to advance and more data becomes available, the field of data science and machine learning is expected to grow and evolve. Here are some emerging trends and future directions:

1.8.1 Deep Learning and Neural Networks

Deep learning, a subfield of machine learning inspired by the structure and function of the human brain, has gained significant attention in recent years. Deep neural networks, with their ability to automatically learn hierarchical representations from raw data, have achieved remarkable success in various domains, including computer vision, natural language processing, and speech recognition. The continued development of deep learning algorithms, along with advancements in hardware capabilities, is expected to drive further breakthroughs in these areas.

1.8.2 Explainable AI and Interpretable Models

As machine learning models become more complex, there is a growing need for transparency and interpretability. Explainable AI (XAI) aims to provide insights into how machine learning models make predictions, helping users understand and trust the results. The development of interpretable models and the integration of explainability techniques into black-box models are active areas of research. This is particularly important in domains where decisions based on machine learning models can have significant consequences, such as healthcare and finance.

1.8.3 Automated Machine Learning (AutoML)

Building and optimizing machine learning models can be a time-consuming and resource-intensive process. Automated Machine Learning (AutoML) aims to automate various steps of the machine learning pipeline, including data preprocessing, feature engineering, model selection, and hyperparameter tuning. AutoML tools and platforms enable non-experts to leverage the power of machine learning without extensive knowledge of the underlying algorithms, making it more accessible to a broader audience.

1.8.4 Federated Learning and Privacy-Preserving Techniques

Privacy concerns surrounding sensitive data have led to the development of privacy-preserving techniques in machine learning. Federated learning is an approach that allows models to be trained on decentralized data sources without sharing the raw data. Instead, models are trained locally on each data source, and only the model updates are shared and aggregated. This approach maintains data privacy while still benefiting from the collective knowledge of the decentralized data sources.

1.9 Applications of Data Science and Machine Learning

Data science and machine learning have found applications in a wide range of industries, revolutionizing processes and decision-making. Here are some notable applications:

1.9.1 Healthcare

Data science and machine learning are transforming the healthcare industry. They are being used for disease diagnosis and prognosis, drug discovery, patient monitoring, and personalized medicine. Machine learning models can analyze large volumes of patient data, including electronic health records, medical imaging data, and genomics data, to identify patterns and make accurate predictions. This can lead to early detection of diseases, more effective treatments, and improved patient outcomes.

1.9.2 Finance

In the financial industry, data science and machine learning are used for fraud detection, credit scoring, algorithmic trading, and risk management. Machine learning algorithms can analyze vast amounts of financial data, including transaction records, market data, and social media sentiment, to identify suspicious activities, assess creditworthiness, make trading decisions, and manage risks. These applications help financial institutions streamline their operations, minimize losses, and provide more accurate and personalized services to their customers.

1.9.3 E-commerce and Marketing

Data science and machine learning have transformed the way businesses engage with customers in the e-commerce and marketing sectors. Recommendation systems, powered by machine learning algorithms, provide personalized product recommendations to customers based on their browsing and purchase history. Sentiment analysis techniques can analyze customer reviews and social media data to gain insights into customer preferences and sentiments. This helps businesses optimize their marketing strategies, improve customer satisfaction, and increase sales.

1.9.4 Transportation and Logistics

The transportation and logistics industry benefits greatly from data science and machine learning. Machine learning models can optimize route planning, predict demand and traffic patterns, and optimize supply chain operations. Predictive maintenance techniques can analyze sensor data from vehicles and machinery to detect anomalies and prevent breakdowns. These applications help transportation and logistics companies reduce costs, improve efficiency, and enhance customer service.

1.9.5 Energy and Utilities

Data science and machine learning are being used in the energy and utilities sector to optimize energy consumption, predict equipment failures, and improve energy grid efficiency. Machine learning models can analyze energy usage patterns and weather data to predict energy demand and optimize energy generation and distribution. Predictive maintenance techniques can analyze sensor data from equipment to detect signs of failure and schedule maintenance proactively. These applications help reduce energy waste, improve reliability, and enhance sustainability.

1.9.6 Manufacturing

In the manufacturing industry, data science and machine learning are used for quality control, predictive maintenance, and supply chain optimization. Machine learning models can analyze sensor data from production lines to detect anomalies and ensure product quality. Predictive maintenance techniques can analyze equipment data to detect signs of failure and schedule maintenance proactively, minimizing downtime. Machine learning algorithms can also optimize inventory management and supply chain operations, reducing costs and improving efficiency.

1.9.7 Natural Language Processing

Natural Language Processing (NLP) is a subfield of data science and machine learning that focuses on the interaction between computers and human language. NLP techniques enable machines to understand, interpret, and generate human language, facilitating applications such as language translation, sentiment analysis, chatbots, and voice assistants. NLP has significant implications in areas such as customer service, healthcare, education, and content generation.

Conclusion

Here, we have explored the fundamental concepts of data science and machine learning. We have discussed the importance of data and how it serves as the foundation for extracting valuable insights. We have also differentiated between supervised and unsupervised learning, highlighting their respective roles in solving different types of problems. Additionally, we have outlined the process of building machine learning models, from data collection to model deployment.

Data science and machine learning have immense potential to transform industries and drive innovation. As businesses and organizations continue to generate and accumulate vast amounts of data, the demand for skilled data scientists and machine learning practitioners will only increase. Understanding the fundamental concepts presented in this chapter provides a solid foundation for further exploration of advanced topics in data science and machine learning.

Data science and machine learning have become fundamental disciplines in the age of big data. Their applications span across various industries, transforming processes, and decision-making. From healthcare to finance, e-commerce to transportation, data science and machine learning are enabling organizations to gain valuable insights, improve efficiency, and deliver better services to their customers.

As data continues to grow in volume and complexity, the need for skilled professionals in data science and machine learning will continue to rise. Understanding the concepts discussed in this chapter provides a solid foundation for individuals to explore the field further and contribute to the advancements and applications of data science and machine learning.

Chapter 2: Foundations of Statistics
Introduction

In the field of data science, having a solid understanding of statistics is paramount. Statistics provides the necessary tools and techniques to analyze and interpret data effectively. This chapter will serve as a comprehensive introduction to the foundations of statistics, covering essential concepts and methods that form the backbone of data analysis.

2.1. Probability

Probability theory is fundamental to statistics and plays a crucial role in understanding uncertainty. Probability measures the likelihood of an event occurring and is represented as a value between 0 and 1, where 0 indicates impossibility, and 1 represents certainty. The basic laws of probability, such as the addition and multiplication rules, govern the relationships between events.

Probability distributions describe the possible outcomes and their associated probabilities in a random experiment. Some commonly used probability distributions include the uniform distribution, normal distribution, binomial distribution, and Poisson distribution. These distributions provide insights into the characteristics of data and help in making statistical inferences.

2.2. Descriptive Statistics

Descriptive statistics involve summarizing and describing data sets using numerical measures and graphical representations. The central tendency measures, such as the mean, median, and mode, provide a summary of the typical or central value of a dataset. The mean is the arithmetic average, the median is the middle value, and the mode is the most frequently occurring value.

Variability measures, such as the range, variance, and standard deviation, quantify the spread or dispersion of the data. The range is the difference between the maximum and minimum values, while the variance and standard deviation measure the average deviation from the mean.

In addition to these measures, graphical representations like histograms, box plots, and scatter plots can visually depict the distribution, shape, and relationships within the data. These descriptive statistics provide a preliminary understanding of the dataset before performing more advanced analyses.

2.3. Inferential Statistics

While descriptive statistics summarize and describe data, inferential statistics involve making inferences and drawing conclusions about a population based on a sample. The population refers to the entire group of interest, while the sample is a subset of the population that is used to represent it.

Sampling techniques, such as simple random sampling, stratified sampling, and cluster sampling, ensure that the sample is representative of the population. Inference relies on the principles of probability and involves estimating population parameters, such as means and proportions, using sample statistics.

Hypothesis testing is a critical component of inferential statistics. It allows us to make decisions and draw conclusions about the population based on sample data. The process involves formulating a null hypothesis and an alternative hypothesis, collecting sample data, and assessing the evidence against the null hypothesis using statistical tests. The p-value, a measure of the strength of evidence against the null hypothesis, determines whether we reject or fail to reject the null hypothesis.

2.4. Statistical Distributions

Statistical distributions provide a mathematical description of the probabilities associated with different outcomes in a dataset. Understanding common distributions is essential for analyzing data and making accurate predictions. Here are a few key distributions:

2.4.1. Normal Distribution:

The normal distribution, also known as the Gaussian distribution, is one of the most important distributions in statistics. It is characterized by its bell-shaped curve and is symmetric around the mean. Many natural phenomena, such as height and IQ scores, follow a normal distribution.

2.4.2. Binomial Distribution:

The binomial distribution models the number of successes in a fixed number of independent Bernoulli trials. It is commonly used when dealing with binary outcomes, such as success/failure or yes/no situations. The distribution is defined by two parameters: the probability of success in a single trial and the number of trials.

2.4.3. Poisson Distribution:

The Poisson distribution models the number of events occurring within a fixed interval of time or space. It is often used to analyze rare events, such as the number of accidents in a day or the number of calls received in an hour. The distribution is characterized by a single parameter, the average rate of occurrence.

2.4.4. Uniform Distribution:

The uniform distribution represents outcomes that are equally likely within a specified range. It is commonly used when there is no prior knowledge or bias towards any specific value.

Understanding the characteristics and properties of these distributions enables data scientists to model and analyze real-world phenomena accurately.

2.5. Statistical Testing and Confidence Intervals

In addition to hypothesis testing, statistical testing involves calculating confidence intervals to estimate population parameters. Confidence intervals provide a range of values within which the true population parameter is likely to fall. The level of confidence, often expressed as a percentage (e.g., 95% confidence interval), determines the width of the interval.

The process of constructing a confidence interval involves selecting an appropriate sample, calculating the sample statistic (e.g., mean or proportion), determining the standard error, and using the appropriate distribution (usually the normal distribution) to find the critical values. The confidence interval is then calculated by adding and subtracting the margin of error from the sample statistic.

Confidence intervals provide valuable information about the precision and reliability of our estimates. A narrower interval indicates higher precision, while a wider interval indicates more uncertainty. The choice of confidence level depends on the desired trade-off between precision and reliability.

2.6. Correlation and Regression Analysis

Correlation analysis examines the relationship between two variables and quantifies the strength and direction of their association. The correlation coefficient, typically represented by the symbol "r," ranges from -1 to 1. A positive value indicates a positive correlation, meaning that as one variable increases, the other variable also tends to increase. A negative value indicates a negative correlation, indicating an inverse relationship.

Regression analysis builds upon correlation analysis and allows us to model the relationship between variables more precisely. It helps predict the value of one variable based on the values of other variables. Simple linear regression involves a single predictor variable, while multiple linear regression incorporates multiple predictor variables.

The regression equation is represented as $y = a + bx$, where y is the dependent variable, x is the independent variable, a is the y-intercept, and b is the slope of the line. The slope represents the change in the dependent variable for a one-unit increase in the independent variable.

Regression analysis provides insights into the strength and significance of the relationship between variables and allows for predictions and forecasting based on the model.

2.7. Experimental Design and Analysis

In many data science applications, experiments are conducted to test hypotheses or evaluate the impact of certain variables. Experimental design involves planning the structure of the experiment to ensure valid and reliable results. Several key considerations include selecting appropriate sample sizes, randomizing the assignment of subjects to treatment groups, and controlling for confounding variables.

Analysis of variance (ANOVA) is a statistical technique used to compare the means of multiple groups in an experiment. It assesses whether there are significant differences between the groups and helps determine which factors contribute to those differences. ANOVA partitions the total variability into different components, such as between-group variability and within-group variability.

Post-hoc tests, such as Tukey's test or Bonferroni correction, are performed following ANOVA to identify specific group differences when there are multiple groups involved.

2.8. Time Series Analysis

Time series analysis focuses on studying data collected at different points in time to understand patterns, trends, and relationships over time. It is widely used in various domains, such as finance, economics, and weather forecasting.

Time series data often exhibit characteristics like trend, seasonality, and autocorrelation. Trend refers to a long-term pattern or direction in the data, while seasonality refers to recurring patterns within a specific time frame, such as daily, monthly, or yearly cycles. Autocorrelation measures the correlation between observations at different time points.

Methods used in time series analysis include moving averages, exponential smoothing, autoregressive integrated moving average

(ARIMA) models, and more advanced techniques like seasonal decomposition of time series (STL) and vector autoregression (VAR) models.

Time series analysis helps in making predictions, identifying anomalies, and understanding the underlying patterns and dynamics within the data.

2.9. Bayesian Statistics

While classical statistics is based on frequentist principles, Bayesian statistics takes a different approach by incorporating prior knowledge and beliefs into the analysis. It provides a framework for updating beliefs based on new evidence.

Bayesian inference involves specifying a prior distribution, which represents our initial beliefs about the parameters of interest, and updating it using Bayes' theorem with the observed data to obtain the posterior distribution. The posterior distribution combines the prior information and the likelihood of the data to provide updated estimates of the parameters.

Bayesian statistics offers advantages such as flexibility in incorporating prior knowledge, the ability to make probabilistic statements about parameters and predictions, and the inclusion of uncertainty measures.

2.10. Ethics and Limitations in Statistics

It is crucial to consider ethical considerations when working with statistics and data analysis. Data scientists must ensure privacy and confidentiality by anonymizing data, obtaining informed consent, and adhering to ethical guidelines and regulations. Ethical concerns also include potential bias in data collection, analysis, and interpretation, as well as the responsible use of data to avoid misleading or harmful conclusions.

Statistics also have limitations. It is essential to recognize that statistical analyses provide insights based on the available data, but they do not guarantee absolute certainty or predictability. Sampling errors, measurement errors, and assumptions made during analysis can impact the validity of results. Therefore, it is crucial to interpret statistical findings with caution and consider the broader context.

2.11. Machine Learning and Statistics

Statistics and machine learning are closely intertwined in the field of data science. While statistics focuses on inference and understanding relationships in data, machine learning emphasizes the development of algorithms that can learn patterns and make predictions or decisions without being explicitly programmed.

Machine learning algorithms rely on statistical principles to train models and make predictions. Techniques such as linear regression, logistic regression, decision trees, random forests, support vector machines, and neural networks all utilize statistical concepts and methods.

Model evaluation in machine learning often involves statistical metrics such as accuracy, precision, recall, F1 score, and area under the curve (AUC). These metrics help assess the performance and generalization capabilities of the models.

Furthermore, statistical techniques play a crucial role in feature selection and dimensionality reduction, which are essential steps in preparing data for machine learning tasks. Methods such as principal component analysis (PCA) and feature importance analysis utilize statistical computations to identify the most relevant features for model building.

2.12. Statistical Software and Tools

In practice, data scientists and analysts utilize various statistical software and tools to implement statistical methods efficiently. These tools provide user-friendly interfaces and a wide range of functions to perform statistical analyses, visualize data, and generate reports.

R is a popular programming language and environment specifically designed for statistical computing and graphics. It offers a vast collection of packages that encompass a wide range of statistical techniques, making it a versatile tool for data analysis and visualization.

Python, another widely used programming language, provides several libraries and packages such as NumPy, Pandas, and SciPy, which offer powerful functionalities for statistical analysis and modeling. Additionally, Python frameworks like scikit-learn and TensorFlow provide robust machine learning capabilities.

Statistical software such as SPSS (Statistical Package for the Social Sciences), SAS (Statistical Analysis System), and Stata are widely used in academic and industry settings for statistical analysis, data management, and reporting.

Data visualization tools like Tableau, Power BI, and matplotlib provide interactive and visually appealing representations of data, facilitating data exploration and communication of results.

2.13. Applications of Statistics in Data Science

Statistics finds applications in various domains and industries, enabling data-driven decision-making and uncovering valuable insights. Here are some key areas where statistics plays a vital role:

2.13.1. Business Analytics:

Statistics helps analyze sales data, customer behavior, market trends, and forecasting demand. It aids in optimizing pricing strategies, identifying target customers, and making informed marketing decisions.

2.13.2. Healthcare and Biostatistics:

Statistical methods are essential in clinical trials, epidemiological studies, and analyzing patient outcomes. They help assess the effectiveness of treatments, detect disease outbreaks, and guide healthcare policies.

2.13.3. Finance and Risk Analysis:

Statistics plays a significant role in portfolio management, risk assessment, and predicting financial market trends. Techniques like regression analysis and time series analysis assist in analyzing stock prices, credit scoring, and fraud detection.

2.13.4. Social Sciences:

Statistics is crucial in social sciences for survey design, sampling techniques, and analyzing survey data. It helps researchers draw inferences about population characteristics, test hypotheses, and understand human behavior.

2.13.5. Manufacturing and Quality Control:

Statistical process control (SPC) techniques are used to monitor and improve manufacturing processes. Statistical quality control methods help identify defects, control variations, and ensure product quality.

2.13.6. Environmental Science:

Statistics assists in analyzing environmental data, climate modeling, and assessing the impact of pollutants. It helps evaluate trends, detect anomalies, and make predictions in areas like weather forecasting and environmental policy.

These are just a few examples of how statistics is applied across different domains. The versatility and wide-ranging applications of statistics make it an indispensable tool in data science.

Conclusion

This chapter has provided an extensive overview of the foundations of statistics in data science. We explored essential concepts such as probability, descriptive and inferential statistics, statistical distributions, and statistical testing. Additionally, we discussed correlation analysis, regression analysis, experimental design, time series analysis, Bayesian statistics, and their applications.

We also touched upon the integration of statistics with machine learning, statistical software and tools, and various real-world applications of statistics in different domains.

Understanding and applying statistics is essential for data scientists and analysts to extract valuable insights from data, build accurate models, make informed decisions, and solve complex problems. By leveraging statistical techniques and tools, data professionals can unlock the power of data and contribute to advancements in diverse fields.

As the field of data science continues to evolve, a solid foundation in statistics will remain a fundamental pillar, enabling data-driven discoveries and innovations.

Chapter 3: Python for Data Science

Introduction

Python has emerged as a popular programming language in the field of data science due to its simplicity, versatility, and extensive library ecosystem. This chapter aims to provide a comprehensive introduction to Python for data science. We will cover the basics of Python syntax, data structures, and key libraries such as NumPy, Pandas, and Matplotlib, which are essential for data manipulation, analysis, and visualization.

3.1. Python Basics

Python is known for its easy-to-understand syntax and readability, making it an excellent language for beginners. Here are some fundamental concepts and features of Python:

3.1.1. Variables and Data Types:

In Python, variables are used to store data values. Python supports various data types, including integers, floats, strings, booleans, lists, tuples, and dictionaries.

3.1.2. Operators:

Python provides a wide range of operators for performing arithmetic, comparison, assignment, logical, and bitwise operations. These operators allow for mathematical computations and logical evaluations.

3.1.3. Control Flow:

Control flow structures such as conditional statements (if-else) and loops (for and while) enable program control and flow based on certain conditions. These structures allow for decision-making and repetitive execution of code.

3.1.4. Functions:

Functions in Python are reusable blocks of code that perform specific tasks. They help modularize code and make it more readable and organized. Python also supports the creation of user-defined functions.

3.1.5. Modules and Packages:

Python's modular nature allows the use of external modules and packages, which are collections of functions and classes that extend Python's capabilities. Modules and packages provide additional functionalities and simplify complex tasks.

3.2. NumPy: Numerical Computing in Python

NumPy (Numerical Python) is a fundamental library for numerical computing in Python. It provides powerful tools for working with multi-dimensional arrays and performing mathematical operations efficiently. Here are some key features of NumPy:

3.2.1. ndarray:

The ndarray (N-dimensional array) is the core data structure of NumPy. It allows for efficient storage and manipulation of large, homogeneous arrays of data. NumPy arrays provide faster computations compared to traditional Python lists.

3.2.2. Array Operations:

NumPy provides a wide range of mathematical and logical operations that can be performed on arrays. These operations include element-wise arithmetic, array broadcasting, aggregation functions, and array slicing.

3.2.3. Linear Algebra:

NumPy offers a comprehensive suite of linear algebra functions, including matrix operations, eigenvalues, eigenvectors, singular value decomposition, and more. These functions enable efficient linear algebra computations in data science applications.

3.2.4. Random Number Generation:

NumPy includes functions for generating random numbers from various probability distributions. This capability is useful for simulations, testing algorithms, and generating random data.

3.2.5. Integration with other Libraries:

NumPy integrates seamlessly with other libraries in the data science ecosystem, such as Pandas and Matplotlib, allowing for efficient data manipulation and visualization.

3.3. Pandas: Data Manipulation and Analysis

Pandas is a powerful library for data manipulation and analysis in Python. It provides data structures and functions to efficiently work with structured and tabular data. Some key features of Pandas include:

3.3.1. Data Structures:

Pandas introduces two primary data structures, the Series and DataFrame, which are designed for easy handling of one-dimensional and two-dimensional data, respectively. These data structures provide flexibility and powerful functionalities for data manipulation.

3.3.2. Data Cleaning and Preprocessing:

Pandas offers a wide range of functions for handling missing data, removing duplicates, handling outliers, and transforming data. These functions allow for data cleaning and preprocessing tasks before analysis.

3.3.3. Data Indexing and Selection:

Pandas provides powerful indexing capabilities to select, filter, and subset data based on various criteria. It allows for both label-based and position-based indexing, making data retrieval and manipulation flexible and efficient.

3.3.4. Aggregation and Grouping:

Pandas supports efficient aggregation operations, such as calculating summary statistics, group-wise computations, and pivot tables. These operations help in gaining insights from data and summarizing information at different levels of granularity.

3.3.5. Data Input and Output:

Pandas facilitates reading and writing data in various formats, including CSV, Excel, SQL databases, and more. It provides seamless integration with different data sources, making data ingestion and export straightforward.

3.4. Matplotlib: Data Visualization in Python

Matplotlib is a comprehensive data visualization library in Python. It enables the creation of a wide range of static, animated, and interactive visualizations. Key features of Matplotlib include:

3.4.1. Plotting Functions:

Matplotlib provides a variety of plotting functions to create line plots, scatter plots, bar plots, histograms, box plots, and more. These functions offer customizable options for colors, markers, labels, and annotations.

3.4.2. Subplots and Figures:

Matplotlib allows for the creation of multiple plots within the same figure using subplots. It supports customization of subplot layouts, axes properties, and figure sizes to create complex visualizations.

3.4.3. Visual Styles and Themes:

Matplotlib supports the customization of visual styles through the use of style sheets and themes. These features allow for the creation of visually appealing and consistent plots.

3.4.4. Annotations and Labels:

Matplotlib enables the addition of text annotations, titles, and labels to plots, making it easier to communicate the intended message. It also supports the inclusion of legends, grids, and other visual elements to enhance plot clarity.

3.4.5. Exporting and Saving:

Matplotlib provides functionalities to export plots in various formats, including PNG, PDF, SVG, and more. It allows for high-quality and publication-ready output for different purposes.

3.5. Other Essential Libraries in Python

Apart from NumPy, Pandas, and Matplotlib, there are several other important libraries that are extensively used in data science projects. Here are a few notable ones:

3.5.1. Scikit-learn:

Scikit-learn is a comprehensive library for machine learning in Python. It provides a wide range of algorithms for classification, regression, clustering, dimensionality reduction, and model evaluation. Scikit-learn offers consistent APIs and tools for model training, validation, and deployment.

3.5.2. TensorFlow and Keras:

TensorFlow is a popular library for deep learning and neural network computations. It provides a flexible framework for building and training deep learning models. Keras, built on top of TensorFlow, offers a user-friendly and high-level API for rapid prototyping of deep learning models.

3.5.3. SciPy:

SciPy is a library that builds on top of NumPy and provides additional scientific computing capabilities. It includes modules for optimization, integration, signal processing, image processing, and more. SciPy complements NumPy and enhances the scientific computing capabilities in Python.

3.5.4. Seaborn:

Seaborn is a data visualization library based on Matplotlib. It offers high-level interfaces for creating attractive and informative statistical graphics. Seaborn simplifies the creation of complex visualizations and provides additional statistical functionality.

3.5.5. StatsModels:

StatsModels is a library focused on statistical modeling and analysis. It offers a wide range of statistical models, hypothesis tests, and statistical tools for exploring and modeling data. StatsModels complements the statistical capabilities of Pandas and provides additional analytical functionalities.

Conclusion

Python has become the language of choice for data scientists due to its simplicity, versatility, and the vast ecosystem of libraries available for data manipulation, analysis, and visualization. This chapter provided an overview of Python's syntax, data structures, and key libraries essential for data science projects.

We explored NumPy, which facilitates efficient numerical computations and provides powerful tools for working with multi-dimensional arrays. Pandas, another essential library, offersflexible data structures and functions for data manipulation and analysis, enabling tasks such as data cleaning, preprocessing, and aggregation. Matplotlib, on the other hand, empowers data scientists to create a wide range of visualizations to effectively communicate insights and findings.

We also touched upon other important libraries such as Scikit-learn for machine learning, TensorFlow and Keras for deep learning, SciPy for scientific computing, Seaborn for advanced data visualization, and StatsModels for statistical modeling and analysis.

Python's simplicity, combined with the capabilities of these libraries, makes it a powerful tool for data scientists to tackle complex data challenges and extract valuable insights. By mastering Python and its associated libraries, data scientists can leverage the full potential of data science techniques and contribute to data-driven decision-making in various domains.

As the field of data science continues to evolve, Python's role in data analysis and machine learning is expected to grow further. Having a strong foundation in Python for data science is essential for any aspiring or practicing data scientist seeking to excel in the fi

Chapter 4: Data Wrangling and Cleaning

Data analysis is a crucial step in deriving insights and making informed decisions. However, data is rarely clean and ready for analysis. It often contains missing values, outliers, or variables that require transformation for optimal model performance. In this chapter, we will explore the process of data wrangling and cleaning, which involves handling missing data, dealing with outliers, and transforming variables.

4.1. Handling Missing Data

Missing data can significantly impact the results of any data analysis. Therefore, it is essential to address missing values appropriately. There are several techniques for handling missing data:

4.1.1. Deletion:

In this approach, we simply delete any rows or columns with missing values. While this is the easiest method, it may result in loss of valuable information if the missing data is not entirely random.

4.1.2. Imputation:

Imputation involves filling in missing values with estimated or predicted values. There are various imputation techniques available, including mean imputation, median imputation, mode imputation, and regression imputation. Mean imputation replaces missing values with the mean of the available data, while median imputation uses the median. Mode imputation replaces missing values with the mode of the variable. Regression imputation predicts missing values based on other variables using regression models.

4.1.3. Multiple Imputation:

Multiple imputation is a more advanced technique that involves creating multiple imputed datasets, where missing values are imputed multiple times. This approach takes into account the uncertainty associated with imputation and produces more accurate estimates compared to single imputation methods.

4.2. Handling Outliers

Outliers are extreme values that deviate significantly from the rest of the data. They can arise due to various reasons, such as measurement errors, data entry errors, or genuinely unusual observations. Outliers can distort statistical analyses and modeling results. Here are some techniques for handling outliers:

4.2.1. Visual inspection:

Visualizing the data using scatter plots, box plots, or histograms can help identify potential outliers. By examining the distribution of the data, we can identify values that appear significantly different from the rest.

4.2.2. Statistical methods:

Statistical methods such as z-score or modified z-score can be used to detect outliers. The z-score measures how many standard deviations an observation is from the mean. Observations with z-scores above a certain threshold (e.g., 3) can be considered outliers. Modified z-score takes into account the median and median absolute deviation (MAD) instead of the mean and standard deviation, making it more robust to outliers.

4.2.3. Winsorization:

Winsorization involves replacing extreme values with less extreme values. For example, we can replace values above a certain threshold with the highest value below that threshold and replace values below a certain threshold with the lowest value above that threshold.

4.2.4. Transformation:

Another approach to handle outliers is to apply transformations to the data. Common transformations include logarithmic transformation, square root transformation, or inverse transformation. These transformations can help make the data distribution more symmetric and reduce the impact of outliers.

4.3. Variable Transformation for Model Performance

In some cases, the relationship between variables and the target variable may not be linear or may not follow the assumptions of the chosen model. In such situations, transforming variables can improve the model's performance. Here are some common variable transformations:

4.3.1. Logarithmic transformation:

The logarithmic transformation is useful when the relationship between variables is multiplicative rather than additive. Taking the logarithm of the variables can help linearize the relationship and make it more suitable for linear models.

4.3.2. Power transformation:

Power transformations, such as square root or cube root transformations, can be applied to stabilize the variance of the data or make the relationship with the target variable more linear.

4.3.3. Box-Cox transformation:

The Box-Cox transformation is a more general transformation method that includes both logarithmic and power transformations. It calculates an optimal power parameter that maximizes the likelihood of the transformed data.

4.4. Feature Scaling

Feature scaling is an essential step in data preprocessing, especially when working with algorithms that are sensitive to the scale of the features. Scaling ensures that all features have a similar range and prevents some variables from dominating others. Here are two common techniques for feature scaling:

4.4.1. Standardization (Z-score normalization):

Standardization scales the data to have zero mean and unit variance. It subtracts the mean of the variable and divides by the standard deviation.

4.4.2. Min-Max scaling:

Min-Max scaling scales the data to a fixed range, typically between 0 and 1. It subtracts the minimum value of the variable and divides by the range (maximum value minus minimum value).

4.5. Dealing with Categorical Variables

In addition to numerical variables, datasets often contain categorical variables, which require special treatment during the data wrangling process. Categorical variables represent qualitative characteristics, such as gender, color, or product type. Here are some techniques for handling categorical variables:

4.5.1. One-Hot Encoding:

One-hot encoding is a popular method for representing categorical variables as binary vectors. It creates new binary columns for each category in the original variable. For example, if we have a variable "Color" with categories red, blue, and green, one-hot encoding would create three binary columns: "IsRed," "IsBlue," and "IsGreen." The corresponding value in each column would be 1 if the observation belongs to that category and 0 otherwise.

4.5.2. Label Encoding:

Label encoding assigns a unique numeric label to each category in the variable. For instance, if we have a variable "Size" with categories small, medium, and large, label encoding would assign the labels 0, 1, and 2 to the categories, respectively. Label encoding is suitable when there is an inherent order or ranking among the categories.

4.5.3. Ordinal Encoding:

Ordinal encoding is similar to label encoding but considers the ordinal relationship between categories. It assigns numeric labels based on the order of the categories. For example, if we have a variable "Education" with categories high school, college, and postgraduate, we can assign the labels 0, 1, and 2, respectively. Ordinal encoding is appropriate when the categories have a natural ordering.

4.5.4. Dummy Encoding:

Dummy encoding is another method for handling categorical variables. It creates binary columns representing each category, but instead of using one-hot encoding, it assigns 0 or 1 to each column. If a particular observation belongs to a specific category, the corresponding binary column will have a value of 1; otherwise, it will be 0. Dummy encoding is useful when dealing with categorical variables with a large number of categories, as it reduces the dimensionality of the data.

4.6. Data Integration and Transformation

In real-world scenarios, data often comes from multiple sources and needs to be integrated before analysis. Data integration involves combining datasets with different structures, formats, or variables into a unified dataset. Here are some techniques for data integration and transformation:

4.6.1. Concatenation:

Concatenation is a simple technique that combines datasets by appending rows or columns. It is suitable when the datasets have the same variables or represent different instances of the same variables.

4.6.2. Joining and Merging:

Joining and merging are techniques used to combine datasets based on common variables. For example, if we have two datasets, one with customer information and another with purchase history, we can join them based on a shared customer ID variable. Joining and merging allow us to create comprehensive datasets that include information from multiple sources.

4.6.3. Aggregation:

Aggregation involves summarizing or reducing the data to a coarser level. It is useful when dealing with large datasets or when the analysis requires higher-level insights. Common aggregation functions include sum, mean, median, count, and maximum.

4.6.4. Feature Engineering:

Feature engineering involves creating new variables (features) based on existing variables. These new features can capture additional information or relationships that are not explicitly represented in the original data. Feature engineering techniques include creating interaction terms, polynomial features, or time-based features.

4.7. Data Cleaning Best Practices

In addition to the specific techniques mentioned above, it is essential to follow some best practices during the data wrangling and cleaning process. Here are a few guidelines:

4.7.1. Documenting Changes:

It is crucial to keep a record of the changes made during the data cleaning process. This documentation helps ensure transparency and reproducibility of the analysis. It also allows other researchers or stakeholders to understand and validate the data cleaning steps.

4.7.2. Handling Data Entry Errors:

Data entry errors are common and can significantly impact the quality of the data. It is essential to carefully check for inconsistencies, misspellings, or incorrect data values. Validating the data against known sources or conducting data audits can help identify and rectify data entry errors.

4.7.3. Dealing with Skewed Distributions:

Skewed distributions, where the data is not evenly distributed, can affect the performance of statistical models. Applying appropriate transformations, such as logarithmic or power transformations, can help normalize the data and improve model performance.

4.7.4. Regular Updating:

Data cleaning is not a one-time process. As new data becomes available or the dataset evolves, it is crucial to regularly update and re-evaluate the data cleaning procedures. This ensures that the analysis is based on the most accurate and up-to-date data.

Conclusion:

Data wrangling and cleaning are indispensable steps in the data analysis process. Handling missing data, outliers, and categorical variables, as well as transforming variables, are essential techniques for preparing the data for analysis. Additionally, integrating and transforming data from different sources and following data cleaning best practices ensure the accuracy and reliability of the analysis. By employing these techniques and adhering to best practices, data analysts can extract valuable insights, build robust models, and make informed decisions based on high-quality data.

Chapter 5: Exploratory Data Analysis

Before embarking on the modeling phase of a data analysis project, it is essential to thoroughly understand the dataset through exploratory data analysis (EDA). Exploratory data analysis allows us to gain insights into the data, uncover patterns, relationships, and anomalies, and inform our modeling decisions. In this chapter, we will explore various techniques to effectively explore and visualize data.

5.1. Understanding Data Distributions

Understanding the distribution of variables in a dataset is fundamental to uncovering valuable insights. Here are some techniques to explore data distributions:

5.1.1. Descriptive Statistics:

Descriptive statistics provide summary measures such as mean, median, mode, standard deviation, and quartiles. These statistics give us a basic understanding of the central tendency, spread, and shape of the data.

5.1.2. Histograms:

Histograms provide a visual representation of the distribution of a continuous variable. They divide the data into bins and display the frequency or count of observations falling within each bin. Histograms help us understand the shape and spread of the data, identify outliers, and detect potential data issues such as skewness or multimodality.

5.1.3. Density Plots:

Density plots are another way to visualize the distribution of a continuous variable. They provide a smooth estimate of the underlying probability density function. Density plots can reveal more nuanced information about the data distribution compared to histograms.

5.1.4. Bar Plots:

Bar plots are useful for visualizing the distribution of categorical variables. They display the frequency or count of observations for each category as bars. Bar plots help us understand the proportions and frequencies of different categories and identify dominant or rare categories.

5.2. Exploring Relationships Between Variables

Exploring the relationships between variables is crucial for understanding dependencies, uncovering patterns, and identifying potential predictive factors. Here are some techniques for exploring relationships between variables:

5.2.1. Scatter Plots:

Scatter plots visualize the relationship between two continuous variables. Each observation is represented as a point on the plot, with one variable on the x-axis and the other on the y-axis. Scatter plots help us identify trends, patterns, and potential correlations between variables. They can also reveal outliers or clusters of data points.

5.2.2. Correlation Analysis:

Correlation analysis measures the strength and direction of the linear relationship between two continuous variables. The correlation coefficient, such as Pearson's correlation coefficient, ranges from -1 to 1, with 0 indicating no correlation, -1 indicating a perfect negative correlation, and 1 indicating a perfect positive correlation. Correlation matrices or heatmaps provide a comprehensive view of the correlations between multiple variables.

5.2.3. Box Plots:

Box plots display the distribution of a continuous variable across different categories or groups. They provide a visual summary of the median, quartiles, and potential outliers. Box plots help us compare the distributions of different groups and identify potential differences or relationships between variables.

5.2.4. Heatmaps:

Heatmaps are effective for visualizing the relationship between multiple variables simultaneously. Heatmaps use color gradients to represent the values of variables in a matrix. They allow us to detect patterns, clusters, or correlations among variables at a glance.

5.3. Identifying Patterns and Outliers

Identifying patterns and outliers is crucial for understanding the underlying structure of the data and detecting potential anomalies. Here are some techniques for pattern identification and outlier detection:

5.3.1. Time Series Analysis:

If the data has a temporal dimension, time series analysis can help identify trends, seasonality, and other temporal patterns. Techniques such as moving averages, autocorrelation plots, and decompositions can provide insights into the underlying patterns and seasonality in the data.

5.3.2. Clustering Analysis:

Clustering analysis is used to group similar observations together based on their characteristics. It helps identify patterns, similarities, or differences among the observations. Clustering algorithms such as k-means or hierarchical clustering can be applied to identify natural groupings within the data.

5.3.3. Outlier Detection:

Outliers are observations that deviate significantly from the majority of the data. Outliers can be identified using statistical techniques such as z-score or modified z-score, which measure how far an observation is from the mean or median of the data. Other methods, such as the Mahalanobis distance or isolation forests, can also be used for outlier detection.

5.3.4. Geospatial Analysis:

If the data includes geographical information, geospatial analysis techniques can be used to explore spatial patterns, clusters, or relationships. Maps, spatial autocorrelation analysis, or spatial interpolation methods can provide valuable insights into the data.

5.4. Visualizing Data

Data visualization is a powerful tool for conveying information, patterns, and insights effectively. Here are some techniques for visualizing data:

5.4.1. Line Charts:

Line charts are useful for visualizing trends and patterns over time or across ordered categories. They connect data points with lines, providing a clear representation of the data's progression.

5.4.2. Bar Charts:

Bar charts are effective for comparing the values of categorical variables or displaying frequencies. They use vertical or horizontal bars to represent each category's value or frequency, allowing for easy comparison.

5.4.3. Pie Charts:

Pie charts are suitable for displaying proportions or percentages of categorical variables. Each category is represented as a slice of the pie, with the size of the slice corresponding to its proportion or percentage.

5.4.4. Heatmaps:

Heatmaps, as mentioned earlier, are powerful for visualizing relationships and patterns among multiple variables. They use color gradients to represent the values in a matrix, allowing for easy identification of patterns or clusters.

5.4.5. Interactive Visualizations:

Interactive visualizations, created using tools such as D3.js or Plotly, provide dynamic and engaging representations of the data. Interactive elements, such as tooltips or filters, allow users to explore the data from different angles, facilitating a deeper understanding of the insights.

5.5. Handling Missing Data in EDA

During exploratory data analysis, it is important to address missing data appropriately. Missing data can skew the analysis and lead to inaccurate conclusions. Here are some techniques for handling missing data during EDA:

5.5.1. Missing Data Visualization:

Before applying any imputation techniques, it is useful to visualize the missing data patterns. Missing data can be visualized using heatmaps or bar plots, where missing values are represented as empty cells or bars. This visualization helps identify variables with high levels of missingness and understand any potential patterns or relationships between missing values.

5.5.2. Missing Data Imputation:

Imputation techniques, discussed in the previous chapter, can be applied during EDA to fill in missing values. This allows us to explore the data as a complete dataset. However, it is important to note that imputation introduces some level of uncertainty, and the imputed values should be interpreted with caution.

5.5.3. Missing Data Indicators:

Instead of imputing missing values, another approach is to create binary indicators to flag missing data. These indicators can be used as additional variables during the analysis to account for the missingness. This approach helps retain the information that data is missing while allowing the exploration of the available data.

5.6. Feature Engineering in EDA

Feature engineering involves creating new variables or transforming existing variables to extract more meaningful information from the data. During EDA, feature engineering can help uncover hidden patterns and relationships. Here are some techniques for feature engineering during EDA:

5.6.1. Creating Interaction Terms:

Interaction terms are variables that capture the combined effect of two or more variables. For example, if we have variables for height and weight, we can create an interaction term by multiplying the height and weight values. This interaction term may provide additional insight into the relationship between height, weight, and the target variable.

5.6.2. Polynomial Features:

Polynomial features involve creating new variables by raising existing variables to higher powers. For example, if we have a variable x, we can create new variables x^2, x^3, and so on. This can help capture nonlinear relationships between variables.

5.6.3. Time-Based Features:

If the data has a time component, creating time-based features can provide valuable insights. Time-based features can include variables such as day of the week, month, season, or time since a particular event. These features can reveal patterns or trends that are specific to certain time periods.

5.6.4. Binning:

Binning involves dividing continuous variables into discrete intervals or bins. This can help simplify the data and reveal patterns that are not apparent when using continuous variables. Binned variables can be analyzed using bar plots or other visualizations.

5.7. EDA for Machine Learning Models

EDA is particularly important when preparing data for machine learning models. It helps in understanding the relationships between variables, identifying relevant features, and selecting appropriate models. Here are some considerations for EDA in the context of machine learning:

5.7.1. Target Variable Analysis:

Analyzing the distribution of the target variable is essential for understanding its characteristics. This includes examining its distribution, checking for class imbalance, and identifying potential outliers. Understanding the target variable guides the choice of appropriate modeling techniques.

5.7.2. Feature Selection:

EDA can help identify relevant features for the machine learning models. By examining the relationships between variables and the target variable, we can select the most informative features for prediction. Feature selection techniques, such as correlation analysis or recursive feature elimination, can be applied during EDA.

5.7.3. Dimensionality Reduction:

If the dataset has a high number of features, dimensionality reduction techniques can be applied during EDA. Techniques like principal component analysis (PCA) or t-SNE can help visualize and reduce the dimensionality of the data, allowing for a more manageable and interpretable representation.

5.7.4. Model Evaluation:

EDA can provide insights into potential challenges or limitations of the chosen machine learning models. By understanding the characteristics of the data, such as class imbalance, outliers, or nonlinear relationships, we can select appropriate evaluation metrics and consider specific modeling techniques that address these challenges.

Conclusion:

Exploratory data analysis is a critical step in the data analysis process, allowing us to gain insights and inform modeling decisions. Techniques such as understanding data distributions, exploring relationships between variables, handling missing data, performing feature engineering, and considering EDA for machine learning models enable us to extract valuable information and patterns from the data. Through effective EDA, analysts can make more informed decisions, build accurate models, and generate actionable insights.

Chapter 6: Supervised Learning: Regression

Regression analysis is a widely used technique in data analysis and machine learning for predicting numerical outcomes. It involves modeling the relationship between a dependent variable (the outcome to be predicted) and one or more independent variables (predictor variables). In this chapter, we will delve into supervised learning algorithms for regression tasks. We will explore linear regression, decision tree regression, and other regression models. We will learn how to train models, evaluate their performance, and interpret the results.

6.1. Introduction to Regression Analysis

Regression analysis is a statistical modeling technique that aims to estimate the relationships between variables. In the context of supervised learning, regression focuses on predicting a continuous numerical outcome. The dependent variable, also known as the target variable, is the variable we want to predict. The independent variables, also known as predictor variables, are the variables used to make the prediction. The goal of regression is to find a mathematical function that best represents the relationship between the predictors and the target variable.

6.2. Linear Regression

Linear regression is one of the most fundamental and widely used regression techniques. It assumes a linear relationship between the predictors and the target variable. In linear regression, the model estimates the coefficients for each predictor variable, representing the slope of the relationship. The model also estimates an intercept term, representing the starting point of the relationship.

6.2.1. Simple Linear Regression:

Simple linear regression involves a single predictor variable. The model can be represented by the equation: $Y = \beta 0 + \beta 1 X + \varepsilon$, where Y is the target variable, X is the predictor variable, $\beta 0$ is the intercept, $\beta 1$ is the coefficient for the predictor variable, and ε is the error term.

6.2.2. Multiple Linear Regression:

Multiple linear regression extends simple linear regression to include multiple predictor variables. The model can be represented by the equation: $Y = \beta 0 + \beta 1 X 1 + \beta 2 X 2 + ... + \beta n X n + \varepsilon$, where X1, X2, ..., Xn are the predictor variables, $\beta 1$, $\beta 2$, ..., βn are the coefficients for the respective predictor variables, and ε is the error term.

6.3. Decision Tree Regression

Decision tree regression is a non-parametric regression technique that builds a tree-like model of decisions and their predicted outcomes. It partitions the data based on predictor variables and constructs decision rules to predict the target variable. Each leaf node of the tree represents a prediction. Decision tree regression is particularly useful when the relationship between the predictors and the target variable is nonlinear or when there are interactions among the predictors.

6.4. Other Regression Models

In addition to linear regression and decision tree regression, there are several other regression models that can be employed for different scenarios. Some of these models include:

6.4.1. Polynomial Regression:

Polynomial regression extends linear regression by including polynomial terms of the predictor variables. It can capture nonlinear relationships between the predictors and the target variable by introducing higher-order terms.

6.4.2. Support Vector Regression (SVR):

SVR is a regression technique that utilizes support vector machines (SVM) to find a hyperplane that maximizes the margin while minimizing the errors. It is particularly effective when dealing with datasets with high dimensionality or non-linear relationships.

6.4.3. Random Forest Regression:

Random forest regression combines multiple decision trees to make predictions. It reduces overfitting and increases accuracy by aggregating predictions from different trees. Random forest regression is robust and can handle a large number of predictor variables.

6.4.4. Gradient Boosting Regression:

Gradient boosting regression is an ensemble method that combines weak learners (decision trees) into a strong predictive model. It iteratively builds a sequence of models, where each model tries to correct the mistakes made by the previous models. Gradient boosting regression often achieves high predictive performance.

6.5. Model Training and Evaluation

To train a regression model, we typically split the dataset into a training set and a test set. The training set is used to fit the model, while the test set is used to evaluate the model's performance. Common evaluation metrics for regression include:

6.5.1. Mean Squared Error (MSE):

MSE measures the average squared difference between the predicted values and the actual values. It penalizes large errors more heavily.

6.5.2. Root Mean Squared Error (RMSE):

RMSE is the square root of the MSE. It provides a measure of the average error in the same units as the target variable.

6.5.3. R-squared (R2):

R-squared represents the proportion of variance in the target variable that is explained by the regression model. It ranges from 0 to 1, where 1 indicates a perfect fit.

6.5.4. Mean Absolute Error (MAE):

MAE measures the average absolute difference between the predicted values and the actual values. It provides a measure of the average error in the same units as the target variable.

6.6. Model Interpretation

Interpreting regression models involves understanding the estimated coefficients and their significance. The coefficients represent the strength and direction of the relationship between the predictor variables and the target variable. Positive coefficients indicate a positive relationship, while negative coefficients indicate a negative relationship. The magnitude of the coefficient represents the extent of the effect. Statistical significance tests, such as p-values, can be used to determine whether the coefficients are significantly different from zero.

Interpreting decision tree regression models involves understanding the decision rules and the splits in the tree. Each split represents a decision based on a predictor variable, and the leaf nodes represent the predicted outcome. The depth and structure of the tree can provide insights into the important predictors and their relationships with the target variable.

6.7. Model Regularization and Hyperparameter Tuning

Regularization techniques can be applied to regression models to prevent overfitting and improve generalization. Regularization methods, such as Ridge regression and Lasso regression, add penalty terms to the loss function to shrink the coefficients and reduce model complexity.

Hyperparameter tuning is the process of selecting the optimal hyperparameters for the regression model. Hyperparameters are settings that are not learned from the data and need to be specified beforehand. Techniques such as grid search or randomized search can be used to systematically search for the best combination of hyperparameters.

Conclusion:

Regression analysis is a powerful technique for predicting numerical outcomes. In this chapter, we explored linear regression, decision tree regression, and other regression models. We learned how to train regression models, evaluate their performance using metrics such as MSE, RMSE, R-squared, and MAE, and interpret the results by examining coefficients or decision tree structures. By understanding and applying these techniques, analysts can build accurate regression models and make informed predictions in various domains and industries.

Chapter 7: Supervised Learning: Classification

Classification is a fundamental task in supervised learning that involves assigning data points to predefined classes or categories. It is widely used in various domains, such as image recognition, spam detection, and disease diagnosis. In this chapter, we will explore different supervised learning algorithms for classification tasks. We will delve into logistic regression, support vector machines (SVM), decision trees, and ensemble methods such as random forests. We will also learn about model evaluation metrics and techniques to handle imbalanced datasets.

7.1. Introduction to Classification

Classification is the process of predicting categorical labels for input data based on previous observations and training data. The input data, also known as features or predictors, represent the characteristics of the observations, while the labels represent the predefined classes or categories. The goal of classification is to find a decision boundary or a function that separates the different classes in the feature space.

7.2. Logistic Regression

Logistic regression is a popular and widely used classification algorithm. Despite its name, logistic regression is primarily used for binary classification tasks, where there are two possible classes. It models the probability of an observation belonging to a particular class using the logistic function. Logistic regression is a linear model that estimates the coefficients for the predictors, and it can be extended to handle multiclass classification tasks using techniques such as one-vs-rest or softmax regression.

7.3. Support Vector Machines (SVM)

Support Vector Machines (SVM) is a versatile classification algorithm that can handle both linear and nonlinear decision boundaries. SVM aims to find the optimal hyperplane that maximally separates the data points belonging to different classes. It maps the data to a high-dimensional feature space and finds the hyperplane that maximizes the margin between the classes. SVM can also handle nonlinear classification by using kernel functions, such as polynomial or radial basis function (RBF) kernels.

7.4. Decision Trees

Decision trees are intuitive and interpretable classification models that use a tree-like structure to make decisions. Each internal node represents a decision based on a specific feature, and each leaf node represents a class label. Decision trees recursively split the data based on different features to maximize the information gain or Gini impurity. Decision trees are prone to overfitting, but techniques like pruning or ensemble methods can help alleviate this issue.

7.5. Ensemble Methods: Random Forests

Ensemble methods combine multiple classification models to improve predictive performance and reduce overfitting. Random forests are one such ensemble method that constructs an ensemble of decision trees. Each tree is trained on a random subset of the data, and the final prediction is obtained by aggregating the predictions of all the individual trees. Random forests are robust, handle high-dimensional data well, and can handle imbalanced datasets.

7.6. Model Evaluation Metrics

Evaluating the performance of classification models is crucial to understand their effectiveness. Several metrics are commonly used for model evaluation:

7.6.1. Accuracy:

Accuracy measures the proportion of correctly classified instances. It is the most straightforward metric but can be misleading for imbalanced datasets.

7.6.2. Precision:

Precision measures the proportion of true positive predictions among the instances predicted as positive. It focuses on the quality of positive predictions.

7.6.3. Recall:

Recall, also known as sensitivity or true positive rate, measures the proportion of true positives correctly identified among all actual positive instances. It focuses on the completeness of positive predictions.

7.6.4. F1 Score:

The F1 score is the harmonic mean of precision and recall. It provides a balanced measure that considers both precision and recall.

7.6.5. Area Under the ROC Curve (AUC-ROC):

AUC-ROC measures the ability of a classification model to distinguish between the positive and negative classes. It plots the true positive rate against the false positive rate, and a higher AUC-ROC indicates better performance.

7.7. Handling Imbalanced Datasets

Imbalanced datasets, where the classes are not represented equally, can pose challenges for classification models. In such cases, the models may be biased towards the majority class and have poor performance on the minority class. Techniques to handle imbalanced datasets include:

7.7.1. Resampling:

Resampling techniques involve either oversampling the minority class or undersampling the majority class to create a balanced dataset. Oversampling techniques include random oversampling or Synthetic Minority Over-sampling Technique (SMOTE), while undersampling techniques randomly remove instances from the majority class.

7.7.2. Class Weighting:

Class weighting assigns higher weights to instances of the minority class during model training. This gives the minority class more importance, and the model pays more attention to correctly classify those instances.

7.7.3. Ensemble Methods:

Ensemble methods, such as random forests, are often effective in handling imbalanced datasets as they can learn from the imbalanced data distribution and balance the predictions.

7.7.3. Cost-Sensitive Learning:

Cost-sensitive learning involves assigning different misclassification costs to different classes. By assigning higher costs to misclassifying the minority class, the model is encouraged to focus on correctly classifying the minority class.

7.8. Model Interpretability

Interpretability of classification models is crucial for understanding their decision-making process and gaining insights. Some models, such as decision trees, are inherently interpretable as they provide clear decision rules. For more complex models like SVM or neural networks, interpretability can be enhanced by analyzing feature importance or using techniques like LIME (Local Interpretable Model-Agnostic Explanations).

Conclusion:

Classification is a key task in supervised learning that involves assigning data points to predefined classes or categories. In this chapter, we explored various supervised learning algorithms for classification tasks, including logistic regression, support vector machines, decision trees, and random forests. We learned about model evaluation metrics such as accuracy, precision, recall, F1 score, and AUC-ROC. Additionally, we discussed techniques to handle imbalanced datasets and enhance model interpretability. By understanding and applying these techniques, analysts can build accurate and interpretable classification models for various real-world applications.

Chapter 8: Unsupervised Learning: Clustering

Unsupervised learning is a branch of machine learning that deals with unlabeled data, where the objective is to discover patterns and structures without predefined class labels. Clustering is a popular technique in unsupervised learning that groups similar data points together based on their characteristics. In this chapter, we will explore various clustering algorithms, including k-means clustering, hierarchical clustering, and DBSCAN. We will learn how to identify clusters in the data and interpret the results.

8.1. Introduction to Clustering

Clustering is the process of dividing a dataset into groups or clusters such that data points within the same cluster are more similar to each other compared to those in different clusters. It is a form of unsupervised learning since there are no predefined class labels. Clustering algorithms aim to identify underlying patterns, relationships, or structures in the data.

8.2. K-means Clustering

K-means clustering is a popular and widely used clustering algorithm. It aims to partition the data into k clusters, where k is a user-defined parameter. The algorithm starts by randomly initializing k cluster centroids and assigns each data point to the nearest centroid. It then updates the centroids based on the mean of the data points assigned to each cluster. This process iterates until convergence, where the centroids no longer change significantly or a maximum number of iterations is reached. K-means clustering is efficient and works well when the clusters are well-separated and have a roughly equal number of data points.

8.3. Hierarchical Clustering

Hierarchical clustering is a versatile clustering algorithm that creates a tree-like structure or dendrogram to represent the relationships between data points. There are two main types of hierarchical clustering: agglomerative and divisive. Agglomerative hierarchical clustering starts with each data point as an individual cluster and merges the closest clusters iteratively until a single cluster remains. Divisive hierarchical clustering starts with all data points in a single cluster and recursively divides them into smaller clusters. The choice of the merging or splitting criterion, such as distance or similarity measures, determines the structure of the dendrogram.

8.4. Density-Based Spatial Clustering of Applications with Noise (DBSCAN)

DBSCAN is a density-based clustering algorithm that identifies clusters based on the density of data points. It defines clusters as dense regions separated by sparser regions. DBSCAN starts with a randomly selected data point and expands the cluster by connecting neighboring points within a specified distance (epsilon) and minimum number of points (min_samples). It continues to grow the cluster until no more points can be added, and then repeats the process with unvisited data points until all data points are assigned to a cluster. DBSCAN is effective in identifying clusters of arbitrary shapes and is robust to noise and outliers.

8.5. Evaluating Clustering Results

Evaluating the quality of clustering results can be challenging in unsupervised learning since there are no ground truth labels. However, several metrics can help assess the performance and interpretability of clustering algorithms:

8.5.1. Silhouette Score:

The silhouette score measures how well each data point fits into its assigned cluster compared to other clusters. It ranges from -1 to 1, with higher scores indicating better-defined clusters and better separation between clusters.

8.5.2. Davies-Bouldin Index:

The Davies-Bouldin index measures the similarity between clusters by considering the distance between cluster centroids and the within-cluster scatter. A lower index indicates better-defined clusters with less overlap.

8.5.3. Calinski-Harabasz Index:

The Calinski-Harabasz index measures the ratio of between-cluster dispersion to within-cluster dispersion. Higher values indicate well-separated and compact clusters.

8.5.4. Visual Interpretation:

Visualizing the clustering results using scatter plots, heatmaps, or other graphical representations can provide insights into the structure and patterns in the data. It can also help identify any limitations or challenges of the clustering algorithm.

8.6. Interpreting Clustering Results

Interpreting clustering results involves understanding the characteristics of the clusters and the relationships between them. Several techniques can aid in interpretation:

8.6.1. Cluster Centroids or Representatives:

For algorithms like k-means clustering, the cluster centroids or representatives can provide information about the average characteristics of the data points within each cluster. Examining the features or variables associated with each centroid can help understand the differences between clusters.

8.6.2. Heatmaps or Dendrograms:

Heatmaps or dendrograms can reveal patterns and relationships between data points or clusters. They can provide insights into similarities or differences based on the values of the variables or the structure of the dendrogram.

8.6.3. Feature Importance or Variable Contributions:

Analyzing the importance of different features or variables within each cluster can help identify the most discriminative characteristics. Techniques such as feature importance or variable contributions, such as PCA or feature selection methods, can aid in this analysis.

8.6.4. Domain Knowledge and Expertise:

Incorporating domain knowledge and expertise is crucial for interpreting clustering results. Experts in the field can provide insights into the meaningfulness of the identified clusters, validate the results, and generate hypotheses for further investigation.

8.7. Preprocessing and Feature Scaling for Clustering

Preprocessing and feature scaling techniques are essential for preparing data before applying clustering algorithms. Techniques such as data cleaning, handling missing values, and feature normalization or standardization can significantly impact the clustering results. It is important to consider the specific requirements of the clustering algorithm and the characteristics of the data.

Conclusion:

Clustering is a powerful technique in unsupervised learning that allows us to discover patterns and structures within unlabeled data. In this chapter, we explored various clustering algorithms, including k-means clustering, hierarchical clustering, and DBSCAN. We learned how to identify clusters in the data and interpret the results using evaluation metrics, visualizations, and domain knowledge. By understanding and applying these techniques, analysts can uncover meaningful insights, identify groups or clusters within the data, and guide decision-making processes in various domains and industries.

Chapter 9: Dimensionality Reduction

Introduction:

High-dimensional data is becoming increasingly common in various fields such as computer vision, genomics, finance, and social networks. However, analyzing and visualizing data with a large number of dimensions can be challenging. This is where dimensionality reduction techniques come into play. Dimensionality reduction methods allow us to represent high-dimensional data in a lower-dimensional space, making it easier to visualize, analyze, and model the data. In this chapter, we will explore principal component analysis (PCA), t-SNE, and other dimensionality reduction methods.

9.1. Understanding Dimensionality Reduction:

Dimensionality reduction is a process that involves reducing the number of variables or features in a dataset while preserving as much information as possible. The main goal is to find a lower-dimensional representation of the data that captures its essential characteristics. By reducing the dimensionality, we can overcome the curse of dimensionality, which refers to the difficulties that arise when working with high-dimensional data, such as increased computational complexity and sparse data.

9.2. Principal Component Analysis (PCA):

Principal Component Analysis (PCA) is one of the most widely used dimensionality reduction techniques. PCA transforms the data into a new coordinate system, where the axes are the principal components. These principal components are linear combinations of the original features and are orthogonal to each other. The first principal component captures the maximum amount of variance in the data, followed by the second, third, and so on. By selecting a subset of the principal components, we can reduce the dimensionality of the data.

PCA can be used for various purposes, including data visualization, noise reduction, feature extraction, and anomaly detection. It has applications in image processing, natural language processing, and recommender systems, among others. However, it assumes that the data is linearly related and that the principal components are ranked in terms of variance explained. It may not be suitable for datasets with nonlinear relationships or when the relative ordering of the principal components is not significant.

9.3. t-SNE:

t-SNE (t-Distributed Stochastic Neighbor Embedding) is a nonlinear dimensionality reduction technique that is particularly effective for visualizing high-dimensional data. Unlike PCA, which focuses on preserving global structure, t-SNE aims to preserve local structure. It achieves this by constructing a probability distribution over pairs of high-dimensional data points and a similar distribution over pairs of their low-dimensional counterparts. It then minimizes the divergence between these two distributions using a gradient descent approach.

t-SNE is commonly used for visualizing clusters and identifying patterns in complex datasets. It has been successfully applied in various domains, such as image analysis, natural language processing, and bioinformatics. However, it can be computationally expensive and sensitive to the choice of hyperparameters, such as perplexity and learning rate.

9.4. Other Dimensionality Reduction Methods:

In addition to PCA and t-SNE, there are several other dimensionality reduction methods worth exploring:

9.4.1. Linear Discriminant Analysis (LDA):

Linear Discriminant Analysis (LDA) is a dimensionality reduction technique that is commonly used in the context of classification problems. LDA seeks to find a lower-dimensional representation of the data that maximizes the separation between different classes. It achieves this by projecting the data onto a subspace that maximizes the ratio of between-class scatter to within-class scatter.

9.4.2. Independent Component Analysis (ICA):

Independent Component Analysis (ICA) is a dimensionality reduction technique that assumes that the observed data are linear combinations of independent sources. It aims to recover these sources by estimating a linear transformation that makes the resulting components as statistically independent as possible.

9.4.3. Non-negative Matrix Factorization (NMF):

Non-negative Matrix Factorization (NMF) is a dimensionality reduction technique that is particularly useful for non-negative data, such as images and text. It decomposes the original data matrix into the product of two lower-rank matrices, where the elements are constrained to be non-negative. NMF has been successfully applied in image processing, topic modeling, and recommendation systems.

9.4.4. Autoencoders:

Autoencoders are neural network models that can be used for unsupervised dimensionality reduction. They consist of an encoder network that maps the input data to a lower-dimensional representation and a decoder network that reconstructs the original data from the reduced representation. By training the autoencoder to minimize the reconstruction error, the network learns a compressed representation of the data.

9.5. Evaluation and Interpretation of Dimensionality Reduction Results:

When applying dimensionality reduction techniques, it is essential to evaluate the quality of the reduced representation and interpret the results. Some common evaluation metrics include explained variance ratio, reconstruction error, and visualization of the reduced data. It is also crucial to assess the impact of dimensionality reduction on downstream tasks, such as classification or clustering.

Interpreting the results of dimensionality reduction can be challenging, especially when dealing with high-dimensional data. Visualizations, such as scatter plots or heatmaps, can help understand the relationships between variables and identify clusters or patterns. It is also useful to examine the contribution of individual features or variables to the reduced representation. Domain knowledge and expertise play a crucial role in interpreting the results and making meaningful conclusions.

Conclusion:

Dimensionality reduction is a valuable tool in the analysis of high-dimensional data. Techniques like PCA, t-SNE, LDA, ICA, NMF, and autoencoders enable us to transform data into lower-dimensional spaces while preserving essential information. These methods aid in visualization, noise reduction, feature extraction, and anomaly detection. Evaluating and interpreting the results of dimensionality reduction are critical steps to ensure the reliability and usefulness of the reduced representation. As high-dimensional data continues to grow in importance, dimensionality reduction techniques will play a vital role in unlocking insights and understanding complex datasets.

Chapter 10: Feature Engineering and Selection

Introduction:

Feature engineering is a crucial step in the machine learning pipeline that involves creating new features or transforming existing ones to improve the performance of predictive models. By engineering informative and relevant features, we can enhance the model's ability to learn patterns and make accurate predictions. In this chapter, we will explore various techniques for feature engineering, including feature scaling, one-hot encoding, feature extraction, and feature selection methods.

10.1. Feature Scaling:

Feature scaling is a preprocessing technique that aims to bring all features to a similar scale. It is particularly important when working with algorithms that are sensitive to the magnitude of the features, such as distance-based algorithms like k-nearest neighbors and support vector machines. Common techniques for feature scaling include:

10.1.1. Standardization:

Also known as z-score normalization, standardization transforms the features such that they have zero mean and unit variance. This is achieved by subtracting the mean of the feature and dividing by its standard deviation.

10.1.2. Min-Max Scaling:

Min-max scaling transforms the features to a specified range, typically between 0 and 1. It subtracts the minimum value and divides by the range of the feature.

Feature scaling ensures that all features contribute equally to the model training process and prevents the dominance of features with larger scales.

10.2. One-Hot Encoding:

One-hot encoding is a technique used to represent categorical variables as binary vectors. Many machine learning algorithms cannot directly handle categorical features, as they require numerical inputs. One-hot encoding solves this problem by creating new binary variables for each category in the categorical feature. Each binary variable represents whether the original feature belongs to a specific category or not.

For example, consider a categorical feature "color" with categories "red," "blue," and "green." One-hot encoding would create three binary variables: "color_red," "color_blue," and "color_green." If an instance has the "red" color, the "color_red" variable would be 1, and the other variables would be 0.

One-hot encoding ensures that the categorical information is properly represented in a numerical format without imposing any ordinality or magnitude assumptions.

10.3. Feature Extraction:

Feature extraction involves creating new features by combining or transforming existing ones. This process aims to capture relevant information and simplify the representation of the data. Feature extraction techniques include:

10.3.1. Polynomial Features:

Polynomial feature extraction involves creating new features by taking the polynomial combinations of the original features. For example, given a feature "x," its polynomial features can be "x^2," "x^3," and so on. This technique allows the model to capture nonlinear relationships between variables.

10.3.2. Text Feature Extraction:

In natural language processing, text feature extraction techniques such as bag-of-words and TF-IDF (Term Frequency-Inverse Document Frequency) transform textual data into numerical representations. These representations enable the utilization of machine learning algorithms on text data.

10.3.3. Dimensionality Reduction Techniques:

As discussed in Chapter 9, dimensionality reduction methods like PCA and t-SNE can be used for feature extraction. By transforming high-dimensional data into a lower-dimensional space, these techniques extract the most informative features while reducing the dimensionality.

Feature extraction helps to uncover hidden patterns, simplify complex relationships, and reduce noise in the data, thereby improving the model's performance.

10.4. Feature Selection:

Feature selection is the process of identifying and selecting the most relevant features for modeling. Selecting the right set of features can reduce overfitting, enhance model interpretability, and improve computational efficiency. Feature selection methods can be broadly categorized into three types:

10.4.1. Filter Methods:

Filter methods assess the relevance of features based on statistical measures or scoring functions. They rank features independently of the chosen machine learning algorithm. Examples of filter methods include correlation-based feature selection and mutual information-based feature selection.

10.4.2. Wrapper Methods:

Wrapper methods evaluate subsets of features by training and evaluating a specific machine learning algorithm. They consider the performance of the algorithm as a criterion for selecting features. Examples of wrapper methods include recursive feature elimination (RFE) and forward/backward stepwise selection.

10.4.3. Embedded Methods:

Embedded methods incorporate feature selection into the model training process. These methods select features while simultaneously optimizing the model's performance. Examples of embedded methods include LASSO (Least Absolute Shrinkage and Selection Operator) and decision tree-based feature importance.

Feature selection helps to reduce the dimensionality of the data, improve model generalization, and enhance the interpretability of the resulting models.

Conclusion:

Feature engineering and selection are essential steps in the machine learning pipeline that can significantly impact the performance and interpretability of predictive models. Techniques like feature scaling, one-hot encoding, feature extraction, and feature selection allow us to create informative representations of the data and identify the most relevant features for modeling. By investing time and effort in feature engineering and selection, we can improve the efficiency and effectiveness of machine learning models in various domains and applications.

Chapter 11: Model Evaluation and Validation

Introduction:

Model evaluation and validation are essential components of the machine learning pipeline. They allow us to assess the performance and reliability of our models, ensuring that they generalize well to unseen data. In this chapter, we will discuss various evaluation metrics, such as accuracy, precision, recall, and F1-score. Additionally, we will explore techniques like cross-validation, hyperparameter tuning, and model selection to ensure the robustness and reliability of our models.

11.1. Evaluation Metrics:

Evaluation metrics provide quantitative measures to assess the performance of machine learning models. The choice of evaluation metrics depends on the specific problem and the nature of the data. Some commonly used evaluation metrics include:

11.1.1. Accuracy:

Accuracy measures the proportion of correctly classified instances out of the total number of instances. It is a simple and intuitive metric but may not be suitable for imbalanced datasets, where the majority class dominates the accuracy.

11.1.2. Precision:

Precision measures the proportion of true positives (correctly predicted positives) out of all instances predicted as positive. Precision is useful when the cost of false positives is high, and we want to minimize incorrect positive predictions.

11.1.3. Recall (Sensitivity or True Positive Rate):

Recall measures the proportion of true positives out of all actual positive instances. Recall is useful when the cost of false negatives (missed positive instances) is high, and we want to minimize false negatives.

11.1.4. F1-score:

The F1-score is the harmonic mean of precision and recall. It provides a balanced measure that considers both precision and recall. The F1-score is useful when we want to find a balance between precision and recall.

11.2. Cross-Validation:

Cross-validation is a technique used to assess the performance of machine learning models on unseen data. It helps to estimate how well the model will generalize to new instances. In cross-validation, the dataset is divided into multiple subsets or folds. The model is trained on a portion of the data and evaluated on the remaining fold. This process is repeated several times, with different folds used for training and evaluation.

Commonly used cross-validation methods include k-fold cross-validation, stratified k-fold cross-validation, and leave-one-out cross-validation. Cross-validation provides a more robust estimate of model performance by reducing the variance introduced by a single train-test split.

11.3. Hyperparameter Tuning:

Hyperparameters are parameters that are not learned from the data but set before the model training process. They control the behavior and complexity of the model. Hyperparameter tuning involves searching for the optimal values of these hyperparameters to achieve the best model performance.

Grid search and random search are common techniques for hyperparameter tuning. Grid search exhaustively searches through a predefined grid of hyperparameter combinations, while random search samples hyperparameter values randomly from a specified distribution. Advanced techniques like Bayesian optimization and genetic algorithms can also be used for efficient hyperparameter tuning.

Hyperparameter tuning helps to find the optimal configuration of the model, improving its performance and generalization ability.

11.4. Model Selection:

Model selection involves comparing and selecting the best-performing model among different algorithms or variations of the same algorithm. It is crucial to choose the model that best fits the problem at hand and produces the most accurate predictions.

Model selection can be performed using various techniques, including cross-validation. By evaluating the performance of different models on multiple folds of the data, we can compare their performance and select the one with the best average performance.

11.5. Validation Strategies:

In addition to cross-validation, there are other validation strategies that can be employed to evaluate the model's performance. These strategies include:

11.5.1. Holdout Validation:

Holdout validation involves splitting the dataset into training and validation sets. The model is trained on the training set and evaluated on the validation set. This approach is simple and fast but may lead to high variance in the performance estimate, especially with small datasets.

11.5.2. Train-Validation-Test Split:

In this approach, the dataset is split into three subsets: training, validation, and test sets. The model is trained on the training set, hyperparameters are tuned using the validation set, and the final model is evaluated on the test set. This strategy provides an unbiased estimate of the model's performance on unseen data.

11.5.3. Stratified Sampling:

Stratified sampling ensures that the distribution of classes in the training and validation/test sets is representative of the overall distribution. This is especially useful when dealing with imbalanced datasets, where the class proportions are uneven.

Conclusion:

Model evaluation and validation are crucial steps in the machine learning pipeline. Evaluation metrics such as accuracy, precision, recall, and F1-score provide quantitative measures to assess the performance of models. Cross-validation helps estimate the model's generalization ability, while hyperparameter tuning ensures optimal model configuration. Model selection allows us to compare and choose the best-performing model among different algorithms. By employing robust evaluation techniques and validation strategies, we can build reliable and effective machine learning models that perform well on unseen data.

Chapter 12: Ensemble Methods

Introduction:

Ensemble methods are powerful techniques that combine multiple individual models to improve predictive performance. By leveraging the diversity and collective wisdom of multiple models, ensemble methods can often outperform a single model. In this chapter, we will explore ensemble techniques such as bagging, boosting, and stacking. We will understand how ensemble methods work and learn how to implement them using popular libraries such as scikit-learn.

12.1. Bagging:

Bagging, short for Bootstrap Aggregating, is an ensemble technique that involves creating multiple subsets of the training data through bootstrapping (sampling with replacement). Each subset is used to train a separate model, typically with the same learning algorithm. The final prediction is obtained by aggregating the predictions of individual models, either by majority voting (classification) or averaging (regression).

Bagging helps to reduce the variance of the model by averaging out the predictions of multiple models trained on different subsets of the data. It is commonly used with decision tree-based models, resulting in ensemble models like Random Forest.

12.2. Boosting:

Boosting is another ensemble technique that aims to sequentially improve the performance of weak learners by focusing on instances that are difficult to classify correctly. Unlike bagging, boosting trains models in a sequential manner, where each subsequent model tries to correct the mistakes made by the previous models.

Popular boosting algorithms include AdaBoost (Adaptive Boosting), Gradient Boosting, and XGBoost (Extreme Gradient Boosting). Boosting algorithms assign weights to instances during training, emphasizing the misclassified instances in subsequent iterations. The final prediction is obtained by combining the predictions of all individual models, typically using weighted voting or weighted averaging.

Boosting can often achieve better performance than bagging by iteratively learning from the mistakes of previous models and focusing on challenging instances.

12.3. Stacking:

Stacking, also known as Stacked Generalization, is an ensemble technique that combines multiple models using a meta-model, often referred to as a blender or a meta-learner. Stacking involves training several base models on the training data and then using their predictions as inputs to train the meta-model.

The base models can be diverse, using different algorithms or variations of the same algorithm. The meta-model learns to combine the predictions of the base models to make the final prediction. Stacking can exploit the complementary strengths of different models and potentially improve the overall performance.

Stacking requires a more complex implementation compared to bagging and boosting, but it offers greater flexibility and potential for improved performance.

12.4. Implementation using scikit-learn:

The scikit-learn library in Python provides convenient implementations of ensemble methods, making it easy to incorporate them into machine learning workflows.

To use bagging, scikit-learn provides the BaggingClassifier and BaggingRegressor classes, which wrap base models and perform bagging. Random Forest, a popular ensemble model, is also available in scikit-learn as RandomForestClassifier and RandomForestRegressor.

For boosting, scikit-learn provides implementations of AdaBoost (AdaBoostClassifier and AdaBoostRegressor) and Gradient Boosting

(GradientBoostingClassifier and GradientBoostingRegressor). XGBoost, a widely used boosting library, has its own Python API and can be integrated into scikit-learn workflows.

Stacking can be implemented using scikit-learn's StackingClassifier and StackingRegressor classes. These classes allow you to specify the base models, the meta-model, and the strategy for combining the predictions.

By leveraging the scikit-learn library, you can easily experiment with ensemble methods and harness their power for improved predictive performance.

Conclusion:

Ensemble methods are powerful techniques that combine multiple models to enhance predictive performance. Bagging, boosting, and stacking are popular ensemble techniques that leverage the diversity and collective intelligence of multiple models. By reducing variance, focusing on difficult instances, and combining model predictions, ensemble methods can often achieve better performance than individual models. The scikit-learn library provides convenient implementations of ensemble methods, making it easy to incorporate them into machine learning workflows. By leveraging ensemble methods, you can build robust and accurate models that excel in various domains and applications.

Chapter 13: Deep Learning and Neural Networks

Introduction:

Deep learning has emerged as a powerful technique within the field of machine learning, revolutionizing various domains such as computer vision, natural language processing, and speech recognition. In this chapter, we will delve into the fundamentals of neural networks, explore deep learning architectures, and discuss popular frameworks like TensorFlow and Keras. We will also dive into convolutional neural networks (CNNs) and recurrent neural networks (RNNs) and examine their applications in the realm of deep learning.

13.1. Neural Networks:

Neural networks are computational models inspired by the structure and functioning of the human brain. They consist of interconnected artificial neurons, also known as nodes or units, organized into layers. Neural networks learn from data by adjusting the connections and weights between neurons to approximate complex functions or mappings.

The basic components of a neural network include input layers, hidden layers, and output layers. Each neuron receives inputs, applies a transformation using an activation function, and passes the output to the next layer. Through a process called backpropagation, neural networks learn by iteratively adjusting the weights based on the errors between predicted and actual outputs.

13.2. Deep Learning Architectures:

Deep learning architectures refer to neural network models with multiple layers, enabling the learning of complex representations from data. These architectures have shown remarkable performance in various domains. Here are two key deep learning architectures:

13.2.1. Convolutional Neural Networks (CNNs):

CNNs are highly effective for image processing and computer vision tasks. They consist of convolutional layers that learn spatial hierarchies of features from images. CNNs employ filters or kernels to convolve over input data, capturing local patterns and features. Max-pooling layers downsample the learned features, reducing spatial dimensions while preserving important information. CNNs are renowned for their ability to automatically extract and learn meaningful features from images.

13.2.2. Recurrent Neural Networks (RNNs):

RNNs are designed to process sequential data, such as time series, text, or speech. They utilize recurrent connections that allow information to persist across different time steps. RNNs are capable of capturing sequential dependencies, making them suitable for tasks like speech recognition, machine translation, and sentiment analysis. However, RNNs suffer from the vanishing and exploding gradient problems, limiting their ability to capture long-term dependencies.

13.3. Deep Learning Frameworks:

Deep learning frameworks provide high-level abstractions and efficient tools for building and training neural networks. Two widely used frameworks are TensorFlow and Keras:

13.3.1. TensorFlow:

TensorFlow is an open-source deep learning framework developed by Google. It offers a comprehensive set of libraries and tools for building and deploying various machine learning models. TensorFlow supports both high-level and low-level APIs, providing flexibility for different levels of abstraction. Its computational graph-based approach enables efficient execution on CPUs, GPUs, and even distributed systems.

13.3.2. Keras:

Keras is a user-friendly deep learning library that acts as an interface to TensorFlow and other backends such as Theano and CNTK. Keras simplifies the process of building and training neural networks, offering a high-level API with a focus on simplicity and ease of use. It provides a wide range of predefined layers, activation functions, and optimizers, enabling rapid prototyping and experimentation.

13.4. Deep Learning Applications:

Deep learning has demonstrated exceptional performance in various domains and applications, including:

13.4.1. Computer Vision:

Deep learning has revolutionized computer vision tasks such as image classification, object detection, and semantic segmentation. CNNs, in particular, have excelled in image-based tasks, achieving state-of-the-art performance on benchmarks like ImageNet.

13.4.2. Natural Language Processing (NLP):

Deep learning has significantly advanced NLP tasks such as language modeling, sentiment analysis, machine translation, and question answering. RNNs, especially variants like Long Short-Term Memory (LSTM) and Gated Recurrent Units (GRUs), are commonly used for sequential data processing in NLP.

13.4.3. Speech Recognition:

Deep learning has made significant contributions to speech recognition systems, enabling accurate transcription and voice-based command systems. RNNs and hybrid models combining CNNs and RNNs have shown great success in speech recognition tasks.

13.4.4. Recommender Systems:

Deep learning techniques, including collaborative filtering and deep neural networks, have improved the performance of recommendation systems by capturing complex user-item interactions and providing personalized recommendations.

Conclusion:

Deep learning and neural networks have transformed the landscape of machine learning, yielding remarkable results in various domains. Neural networks, with their interconnected artificial neurons, learn complex functions from data through backpropagation. Deep learning architectures such as CNNs and RNNs enable the extraction of meaningful features from images and sequential data. TensorFlow and Keras are popular frameworks that provide powerful tools for building and training neural networks. Deep learning finds applications in computer vision, NLP, speech recognition, and recommender systems, among others. By leveraging deep learning techniques, researchers and practitioners can tackle complex problems and achieve state-of-the-art performance in diverse domains.

Chapter 14: Natural Language Processing

Introduction:

Natural Language Processing (NLP) is a field of artificial intelligence that focuses on enabling machines to understand, interpret, and generate human language. NLP techniques play a crucial role in various applications, such as sentiment analysis, text classification, machine translation, and chatbots. In this chapter, we will explore fundamental NLP techniques, including text preprocessing, sentiment analysis, and text classification. Additionally, we will delve into advanced language models like Word2Vec and transformer models like BERT.

14.1. Text Preprocessing:

Text preprocessing is an essential step in NLP that involves cleaning and transforming raw text data into a format suitable for further analysis. Common text preprocessing techniques include:

14.1.1. Tokenization:

Tokenization involves splitting the text into individual words or tokens. It helps to break down the text into meaningful units for analysis.

14.1.2. Stop Word Removal:

Stop words are common words that often do not carry significant meaning in a given context (e.g., "the," "is," "and"). Removing stop words can reduce noise and improve computational efficiency.

14.1.3. Stemming and Lemmatization:

Stemming and lemmatization are techniques used to reduce words to their base or root form. Stemming involves removing affixes from words (e.g., "running" to "run"), while lemmatization considers the morphological analysis of words and produces the base form (e.g., "better" to "good").

14.1.4. Removing Punctuation and Special Characters:

Removing punctuation marks and special characters helps in reducing noise and simplifying the text data.

Text preprocessing ensures that the text data is in a clean and standardized format for subsequent NLP tasks.

14.2. Sentiment Analysis:

Sentiment analysis, also known as opinion mining, is a common NLP task that aims to determine the sentiment or emotion expressed in a piece of text. It involves classifying text as positive, negative, or neutral. Sentiment analysis can be performed using various approaches, including:

14.2.1. Rule-Based Methods:

Rule-based methods use predefined linguistic rules or lexicons to assign sentiment labels to text. These rules are based on sentiment-related words and patterns. For example, counting the number of positive and negative words in a sentence can determine its sentiment.

14.2.2. Machine Learning-Based Methods:

Machine learning algorithms, such as Naive Bayes, Support Vector Machines (SVM), or Recurrent Neural Networks (RNNs), can be trained on labeled data to classify sentiment. These methods learn patterns and relationships in the data and generalize to unseen text.

Sentiment analysis finds applications in social media monitoring, customer feedback analysis, brand reputation management, and more.

14.3. Text Classification:

Text classification is the process of assigning predefined categories or labels to text documents. It is a fundamental NLP task with various applications, such as spam detection, topic classification, and sentiment analysis. Common approaches to text classification include:

14.3.1. Bag-of-Words (BoW):

The bag-of-words model represents text as a collection of words or tokens, ignoring grammar and word order. It creates a feature vector that counts the occurrence or frequency of each word in the document. Machine learning algorithms can then be trained on these feature vectors for classification.

14.3.2. Term Frequency-Inverse Document Frequency (TF-IDF):

TF-IDF is a numerical statistic that reflects the importance of a word in a document relative to a collection of documents. It combines term frequency (how often a word appears in a document) and inverse document frequency (how rare a word is across documents) to assign weights to words. TF-IDF is often used to represent text data in classification tasks.

14.3.3. Deep Learning Approaches:

Deep learning models, such as convolutional neural networks (CNNs) and recurrent neural networks (RNNs), have achieved great success in text classification. These models can learn complex representations of text and capture contextual information.

14.4. Advanced Language Models:

Advanced language models have revolutionized NLP by capturing rich semantic and contextual information. Two notable models are Word2Vec and BERT:

14.4.1. Word2Vec:

Word2Vec is a neural network-based model that represents words as dense vectors in a continuous vector space. It captures semantic relationships between words and enables mathematical operations on word vectors, such as computing word similarities and analogies. Word2Vec has been widely used for tasks like word embeddings, sentiment analysis, and named entity recognition.

14.4.2. BERT (Bidirectional Encoder Representations from Transformers):

BERT is a transformer-based model that utilizes a transformer architecture to capture contextual information bidirectionally. It has achieved state-of-the-art performance in various NLP tasks, including question answering, natural language inference, and named entity recognition. BERT can be fine-tuned on specific tasks, making it highly adaptable and powerful.

Conclusion:

Natural Language Processing (NLP) techniques enable machines to understand and interpret human language, opening up a wide range of applications. Text preprocessing techniques clean and transform raw text data into a suitable format for analysis. Sentiment analysis allows the classification of text into positive, negative, or neutral sentiments. Text classification assigns predefined categories or labels to text documents, enabling tasks like spam detection and topic classification. Advanced language models like Word2Vec and BERT capture semantic relationships and contextual information, revolutionizing NLP tasks. By leveraging NLP techniques and models, researchers and practitioners can extract valuable insights from text data, improve customer experiences, and enhance various applications involving human language.

Chapter 15: Time Series Analysis

Introduction:

Time series analysis is a field of study that focuses on analyzing and forecasting data points collected over time. Time series data is prevalent in numerous domains, including finance, economics, weather forecasting, and stock market analysis. This chapter will cover essential techniques used in time series analysis, including data decomposition, trend analysis, and popular forecasting models such as ARIMA (AutoRegressive Integrated Moving Average) and LSTM (Long Short-Term Memory).

15.1. Time Series Data:

Time series data consists of observations recorded over regular intervals of time. It is characterized by the temporal ordering of data points, making it different from other types of data. Common examples of time series data include stock prices, weather measurements, and economic indicators. Time series data often exhibits patterns, trends, seasonality, and irregularities that require specialized techniques for analysis.

15.2. Data Decomposition:

Data decomposition is a fundamental step in time series analysis that involves separating a time series into its individual components. The primary components of a time series include:

15.2.1. Trend:

The trend component represents the long-term systematic change in the data over time. It indicates the overall direction of the series, whether it is increasing, decreasing, or stable.

15.2.2. Seasonality:

Seasonality refers to repeating patterns or fluctuations that occur at regular intervals within the time series. These patterns may occur daily, monthly, quarterly, or annually and can be influenced by factors like weather, holidays, or economic cycles.

15.2.3. Residuals or Error:

The residual component represents the random fluctuations or noise that cannot be explained by the trend or seasonality. It captures the irregularities or unexplained variability in the data.

By decomposing a time series into its components, analysts gain insights into the underlying patterns and can make more accurate forecasts.

15.3. Trend Analysis:

Trend analysis aims to identify and analyze the long-term direction or behavior of a time series. It helps understand whether the series is increasing, decreasing, or stationary. Trend analysis techniques include:

15.3.1. Moving Averages:

Moving averages smooth out fluctuations and highlight the underlying trend. The moving average is calculated by averaging a specified number of consecutive data points. Different moving average window sizes can be used to capture short-term or long-term trends.

15.3.2. Regression Analysis:

Regression analysis can be used to fit a linear or non-linear regression model to the time series data. This helps estimate the trend component and understand its relationship with time.

15.3.3. Exponential Smoothing:

Exponential smoothing techniques assign exponentially decreasing weights to past observations to estimate the trend component. It places more weight on recent data points and less weight on older observations.

15.4. Forecasting Models:

Forecasting models are used to predict future values or trends in a time series based on historical data. Two popular forecasting models for time series analysis are ARIMA and LSTM:

15.4.1. ARIMA (AutoRegressive Integrated Moving Average):

ARIMA models capture both autoregressive (AR) and moving average (MA) components in a time series. The model considers the relationship between an observation and a linear combination of lagged observations and moving average terms. ARIMA models are effective for stationary time series and can handle trends and seasonality through differencing.

15.4.2. LSTM (Long Short-Term Memory):

LSTM is a type of recurrent neural network (RNN) that can model and predict sequential data, making it suitable for time series analysis. LSTM networks have memory cells that can capture long-term dependencies and temporal patterns in the data. They are particularly useful when dealing with complex temporal relationships or when the time series exhibits non-linear behavior.

Forecasting models can be trained using historical data and used to predict future values or trends in the time series.

Conclusion:

Time series analysis plays a vital role in understanding and predicting data points collected over time. By decomposing time series data into its components, such as trend, seasonality, and residuals, analysts gain insights into the underlying patterns. Trend analysis techniques help identify and analyze the long-term behavior of the series. Forecasting models like ARIMA and LSTM enable predictions of future values based on historical data. With the advancements in data analysis and deep learning techniques, time series analysis continues to evolve, providing valuable insights and accurate forecasts in various domains such as finance, economics, and weather forecasting.

Chapter 16: Recommender Systems

Introduction:

Recommender systems have become an essential component of modern online platforms, helping users discover relevant and personalized content. These systems analyze user preferences and behaviors to generate recommendations that match individual tastes and interests. In this chapter, we will explore two common types of recommender systems: collaborative filtering and content-based systems. We will learn how to build recommendation engines that provide personalized recommendations to users.

16.1. Collaborative Filtering:

Collaborative filtering is a popular approach in recommender systems that leverages the collective behavior of users to generate recommendations. It assumes that users with similar preferences in the past will have similar preferences in the future. Collaborative filtering techniques can be broadly categorized into two types:

16.1.1. User-Based Collaborative Filtering:

User-based collaborative filtering recommends items to a user based on the preferences of users with similar tastes. It identifies users who have rated or interacted with similar items and suggests items that the target user has not yet experienced.

16.1.2. Item-Based Collaborative Filtering:

Item-based collaborative filtering recommends items to a user based on the similarity between items. It identifies items that are similar in terms of user ratings or interactions and suggests items that are similar to those the target user has already rated or interacted with.

Collaborative filtering does not require explicit knowledge about the content or characteristics of items, making it particularly useful in situations where item attributes are not readily available.

16.2. Content-Based Recommender Systems:

Content-based recommender systems make recommendations based on the characteristics and attributes of items. They analyze the content or features of items and recommend similar items to users based on their preferences. Key steps in building content-based systems include:

16.2.1. Item Representation:

Content-based systems require a representation of items based on their attributes or features. These attributes can include textual descriptions, genre, metadata, or any other relevant information about the items.

16.2.2. User Profile Creation:

User profiles are created based on their interactions or preferences for specific item attributes. This can be done by analyzing their previous interactions, ratings, or explicit feedback.

16.2.3. Recommendation Generation: Recommendations are generated by matching user profiles with item attributes. Similarity measures, such as cosine similarity or Jaccard similarity, are used to compute the similarity between user profiles and item attributes. Items with higher similarity scores are recommended to the user.

Content-based systems are effective when item attributes are available and can be easily extracted or represented.

16.3. Hybrid Recommender Systems:

Hybrid recommender systems combine multiple approaches, such as collaborative filtering and content-based techniques, to provide more accurate and diverse recommendations. By leveraging the strengths of different methods, hybrid systems can overcome limitations and improve recommendation quality. Some common hybrid approaches include:

16.3.1. Weighted Hybrid:

In this approach, recommendations from different techniques are combined by assigning weights to each recommendation source. The weights can be determined based on the performance or reliability of the techniques.

16.3.2. Switching Hybrid:

Switching hybrid systems dynamically select the most suitable recommendation technique based on specific conditions or user preferences. For example, if sufficient user data is available, collaborative filtering might be used; otherwise, a content-based approach can be employed.

16.3.3. Feature Combination:

Feature combination approaches combine both user and item features to create a comprehensive representation of user-item interactions. This combined feature representation can be used for recommendation generation.

16.4. Evaluation of Recommender Systems:

Evaluation of recommender systems is crucial to assess their performance and understand the quality of recommendations. Common evaluation metrics for recommender systems include:

16.4.1. Precision and Recall:

Precision measures the proportion of relevant items among the recommended items, while recall measures the proportion of relevant items that are successfully recommended. These metrics are particularly useful when the focus is on finding relevant items rather than the entire list of recommendations.

16.4.2. Mean Average Precision (MAP):

MAP is a metric that computes the average precision across different levels of recall. It provides a comprehensive measure of recommendation quality.

16.4.3. Normalized Discounted Cumulative Gain (NDCG):

NDCG measures the effectiveness of recommendations by assigning higher weights to top-ranked items. It considers both the relevance and ranking of recommended items.

Evaluation metrics provide insights into the effectiveness and performance of recommender systems, allowing for iterative improvements and optimizations.

Conclusion:

Recommender systems have transformed the way users discover content and products in online platforms. Collaborative filtering leverages the behavior of similar users or items to generate recommendations, while content-based systems analyze item attributes to provide personalized suggestions. Hybrid systems combine multiple approaches to improve recommendation quality. Evaluating recommender systems is crucial to assess their performance and understand the quality of recommendations. By building effective and accurate recommender systems, online platforms can enhance user experiences, increase engagement, and drive customer satisfaction.

Chapter 17: Anomaly Detection

Introduction:

Anomaly detection is a critical task in various domains, including cybersecurity, fraud detection, and industrial monitoring. It involves identifying unusual patterns or outliers in data that deviate significantly from the expected behavior. In this chapter, we will explore different techniques for anomaly detection, including statistical methods, clustering-based approaches, and machine learning-based approaches. We will discuss real-world applications of anomaly detection and the challenges associated with detecting anomalies.

17.1. Statistical Methods:

Statistical methods form the basis for many anomaly detection techniques. These methods assume that normal data follows a specific statistical distribution, and anomalies deviate significantly from this distribution. Common statistical methods for anomaly detection include:

17.1.1. Z-Score or Standard Score:

The z-score measures the number of standard deviations an observation is from the mean. Data points with a z-score above a certain threshold are considered anomalies.

17.1.2. Gaussian Distribution:

Assuming that the data follows a Gaussian or normal distribution, anomalies can be identified by calculating the probability density function (PDF) and identifying data points with a low probability.

17.1.3. Quantile-Based Methods:

Quantile-based methods, such as the Interquartile Range (IQR), identify anomalies based on values that fall outside a specified range, typically defined by percentiles.

Statistical methods are relatively simple and interpretable, making them suitable for detecting anomalies in certain types of data.

17.2. Clustering-Based Approaches:

Clustering-based approaches detect anomalies by identifying data points that do not conform to the typical clusters or groups. These methods assume that anomalies are significantly distant from the normal clusters. Two common clustering-based techniques for anomaly detection are:

17.2.1. Density-Based Spatial Clustering of Applications with Noise (DBSCAN):

DBSCAN groups data points based on their density, considering points that are close together as a cluster. Anomalies are identified as data points that do not belong to any cluster or are located in low-density regions.

17.2.2. Local Outlier Factor (LOF):

LOF calculates the density of a data point relative to its neighboring points. Anomalies are identified as data points with a significantly lower density compared to their neighbors.

Clustering-based approaches can handle complex and high-dimensional data, but their performance may depend on the appropriate choice of clustering algorithms and parameter settings.

17.3. Machine Learning-Based Approaches:

Machine learning-based approaches for anomaly detection utilize algorithms that learn from data to identify abnormal patterns. These methods often require labeled training data, where anomalies are explicitly marked. Common machine learning-based techniques for anomaly detection include:

17.3.1. Support Vector Machines (SVM):

SVMs can be used for both supervised and unsupervised anomaly detection. In unsupervised settings, SVMs separate normal data from the rest, identifying anomalies as outliers.

17.3.2. Isolation Forest:

The Isolation Forest algorithm constructs isolation trees to separate anomalies from normal instances. It measures the number of partitions required to isolate an instance, with anomalies requiring fewer partitions.

17.3.3. Autoencoders:

Autoencoders are neural networks trained to reconstruct input data. Anomalies are identified as data points with high reconstruction error, indicating that they deviate significantly from the normal patterns.

Machine learning-based approaches can handle complex data and adapt to different types of anomalies. However, they may require a considerable amount of labeled training data and careful selection of appropriate algorithms and hyperparameters.

17.4. Real-World Applications and Challenges:

Anomaly detection has numerous real-world applications, including:

17.4.1. Cybersecurity:

Anomaly detection is crucial for detecting and preventing cyber attacks. It helps identify unusual network traffic, system intrusions, or malicious activities that deviate from normal behavior.

17.4.2. Fraud Detection:

Anomaly detection plays a significant role in detecting fraudulent transactions, such as credit card fraud or insurance fraud. It helps identify unusual patterns or behaviors that indicate fraudulent activity.

17.4.3. Industrial Monitoring:

Anomaly detection is used in various industries to monitor equipment, machinery, or processes for abnormal behavior. It helps identify potential faults, failures, or deviations that may lead to safety hazards or operational inefficiencies.

Challenges in anomaly detection include defining what constitutes normal behavior, dealing with high-dimensional and noisy data, handling concept drift (evolving patterns), and avoiding false positives and false negatives. Building robust and accurate anomaly detection systems requires careful consideration of these challenges.

Conclusion:

Anomaly detection is a crucial task in various domains to identify unusual patterns or outliers in data. Statistical methods, clustering-based approaches, and machine learning-based approaches offer different techniques for detecting anomalies. Real-world applications of anomaly detection span cybersecurity, fraud detection, and industrial monitoring. However, anomaly detection comes with challenges such as defining normal behavior, handling noisy data, and avoiding false positives and false negatives. By leveraging appropriate anomaly detection techniques and addressing these challenges, organizations can enhance security, detect fraud, and improve operational efficiency.

Chapter 18: Deploying Machine Learning Models

Introduction:

Deploying machine learning models into production is a crucial step in leveraging the predictive power of these models in real-world applications. Deploying a model involves considerations beyond the modeling itself, including creating APIs for model deployment, model serving, scalability, and integration with existing systems. In this chapter, we will explore various aspects of deploying machine learning models, including frameworks like Flask and Django for creating APIs.

18.1. Model Deployment:

Model deployment refers to the process of making a trained machine learning model available for use in a production environment. When deploying a model, several factors need to be taken into account:

18.1.1. Environment:

Models need to be deployed in an environment suitable for the specific use case. This could include cloud platforms, on-premises servers, or edge devices, depending on the requirements and constraints of the application.

18.1.2. Compatibility:

Ensuring that the deployed model is compatible with the target environment is crucial. This involves considering the hardware, software dependencies, and version compatibility with the deployed model.

18.1.3. Packaging:

Models need to be packaged appropriately for deployment. This includes bundling the model's code, dependencies, and any other necessary files or resources required for its execution.

18.2. Model Serving:

Model serving involves exposing the deployed model as an API to receive input data and provide predictions or responses. Several frameworks and tools can be used to create APIs for model serving:

18.2.1. Flask:

Flask is a lightweight web framework for Python that enables the creation of APIs with ease. It provides a flexible and minimalistic approach to building web applications, making it suitable for serving machine learning models.

18.2.2. Django:

Django is a more comprehensive web framework for Python that provides additional features and functionalities compared to Flask. It includes built-in features like user authentication, database integration, and more, which can be useful for complex applications that involve model serving.

18.2.3. FastAPI:

FastAPI is a modern, fast, and easy-to-use web framework for building APIs with Python. It combines high performance with intuitive development and automatic validation of request and response data.

These frameworks facilitate the creation of RESTful APIs that expose the machine learning model for prediction requests.

18.3. Scalability:

Scalability is a critical aspect of deploying machine learning models, particularly in scenarios with high traffic or large datasets. Ensuring that the deployed model can handle increasing loads and large volumes of data is essential. Techniques for achieving scalability in model deployment include:

18.3.1. Load Balancing:

Load balancing distributes incoming requests across multiple instances or servers to prevent overloading and ensure high availability. This helps in handling increased traffic and improving response times.

18.3.2. Horizontal Scaling:

Horizontal scaling involves adding more instances or servers to the deployment infrastructure to accommodate increased demand. This can be achieved by deploying the model on multiple machines and load balancing the incoming requests.

18.3.3. Containerization:

Containerization technologies like Docker enable packaging the model and its dependencies into portable containers. Containers provide a consistent and isolated runtime environment, making it easier to scale the deployment by spinning up multiple container instances.

18.4. Integration with Existing Systems:

Deploying machine learning models often involves integrating them with existing systems or workflows. This may require connecting the model API to databases, data streaming platforms, or other services. It is crucial to ensure smooth integration and data flow between different components of the system.

Conclusion:

Deploying machine learning models into production involves considerations beyond modeling, including model deployment, model serving, scalability, and integration with existing systems. Frameworks like Flask, Django, and FastAPI facilitate the creation of APIs for model serving. Scalability is essential to handle increasing loads and large volumes of data, and techniques such as load balancing, horizontal scaling, and containerization can be employed. Integrating deployed models with existing systems requires seamless integration and data flow between different components. By addressing these considerations, organizations can effectively deploy machine learning models, leverage their predictive power in real-world applications, and deliver value to end-users.

Chapter 19: Ethical Considerations in Data Science

Introduction:

As data scientists, it is crucial to recognize and address the ethical implications of our work. The field of data science has the potential to impact individuals, communities, and society as a whole. This chapter will delve into various ethical considerations in data science, including privacy, bias, and fairness. We will explore techniques to address bias and ensure fairness in machine learning models.

19.1. Privacy:

Privacy is a critical ethical consideration when working with data. Data scientists must handle personal and sensitive information responsibly to protect individuals' privacy rights. Some key privacy considerations include:

19.1.1. Data Collection:

Ensuring that data collection is conducted transparently and with proper consent from individuals. Data should be collected for specific purposes, and unnecessary or excessive data collection should be avoided.

19.1.2. Data Anonymization and De-identification:

Anonymizing or de-identifying data is essential to protect individuals' privacy. This involves removing or encrypting personally identifiable information (PII) to prevent the identification of individuals.

19.1.3. Data Security:

Implementing robust security measures to protect data from unauthorized access, breaches, and other security risks. This includes encryption, access controls, and regular security audits.

19.2. Bias and Fairness:

Bias in data and machine learning models can lead to unfair outcomes and perpetuate societal inequalities. It is important to identify and address bias to ensure fairness. Considerations for addressing bias and fairness include:

19.2.1. Bias in Data:

Analyzing the data used to train machine learning models for potential biases. Biases can arise from historical societal discrimination or underrepresentation of certain groups. It is essential to recognize and mitigate these biases during data preprocessing.

19.2.2. Algorithmic Bias:

Assessing machine learning models for algorithmic bias. This involves identifying biases that may arise from biased training data, biased features, or biased model behavior. Techniques such as fairness-aware learning, bias mitigation, and model interpretability can help reduce algorithmic bias.

19.2.3. Fairness Metrics and Evaluation:

Defining fairness metrics to evaluate the performance and fairness of machine learning models. Fairness metrics help assess disparities in model predictions across different groups and identify potential sources of unfairness.

19.3. Explainability and Transparency:

Machine learning models should strive to be explainable and transparent, especially in contexts where decisions can have significant impacts on individuals' lives. Techniques for promoting explainability and transparency include:

19.3.1. Interpretable Models:

Using interpretable models, such as decision trees or linear models, that can provide insights into how the model arrives at predictions. This facilitates understanding and trust in the model's decision-making process.

19.3.2. Model Documentation:

Documenting the model's design, data sources, assumptions, and limitations. Transparent documentation helps stakeholders understand the model's capabilities and potential biases.

19.3.3. Model Auditing and Monitoring:

Regularly auditing and monitoring deployed models to ensure they continue to perform as expected and remain fair and unbiased. Ongoing monitoring helps identify and address issues that may arise over time.

19.4. Ethical Decision-Making Frameworks:

Developing and following ethical decision-making frameworks can guide data scientists in addressing ethical considerations. Some commonly used frameworks include:

19.4.1. The Fair Information Practices Principles (FIPPs):

FIPPs outline principles for ensuring fair and responsible data practices, including notice and consent, purpose specification, data minimization, and data integrity.

19.4.2. The Ethical, Legal, and Social Implications (ELSI) Framework:

ELSI frameworks consider ethical, legal, and social implications in research and development processes. It encourages considering the broader societal impacts of data science projects.

19.4.3. The Hippocratic Oath for Data Scientists:

Inspired by the medical profession's Hippocratic Oath, this oath emphasizes a commitment to the responsible and ethical use of data, including protecting privacy, ensuring fairness, and prioritizing the well-being of individuals.

Conclusion:

Ethical considerations in data science are paramount to ensure responsible and fair use of data and machine learning models. Privacy concerns should be addressed by transparent data collection practices, anonymization, and robust security measures. Bias and fairness considerations involve identifying and mitigating biases in data and models to ensure equitable outcomes. Explainability and transparency help build trust in machine learning models and promote accountability. Ethical decision-making frameworks provide guidance for navigating ethical considerations in data science projects. By incorporating ethical considerations into our work, data scientists can contribute to the development of responsible and beneficial applications of data science for individuals and society as a whole.

Chapter 20: Future Trends and Advances in Data Science and Machine Learning

Introduction:

Data science and machine learning are dynamic fields that continually evolve with advancements in technology and research. In this final chapter, we will explore some emerging trends and advances that are shaping the future of data science and machine learning. These trends include explainable AI, federated learning, and automated machine learning (AutoML).

20.1. Explainable AI:

Explainable AI (XAI) focuses on developing machine learning models and techniques that can provide transparent and interpretable explanations for their predictions or decisions. XAI is gaining importance as the need for model transparency and accountability grows. Some techniques used in XAI include:

20.1.1. Rule-Based Models:

Rule-based models, such as decision trees and rule lists, provide interpretable representations that explain the decision-making process based on a set of rules or conditions.

20.1.2. Feature Importance and Shapley Values:

These techniques help identify the features or input variables that contribute most to the model's predictions. They provide insights into the factors influencing the model's decision.

20.1.3. Local Interpretable Model-Agnostic Explanations (LIME):

LIME provides explanations for individual predictions by approximating the model's behavior locally. It highlights the most influential features for a particular prediction.

Explainable AI promotes transparency, trust, and accountability in machine learning models, enabling stakeholders to understand and validate model decisions.

20.2. Federated Learning:

Federated learning is a distributed approach to machine learning that enables model training on decentralized data sources without sharing the raw data. In federated learning, models are trained collaboratively across multiple devices or edge devices, preserving data privacy. Key benefits of federated learning include:

20.2.1. Privacy Preservation:

Federated learning allows training models on data that remains on users' devices, protecting sensitive information and maintaining privacy.

20.2.2. Decentralized Learning:

By distributing the model training process, federated learning enables efficient utilization of local computing resources and reduces the need for data transfer to a central server.

20.2.3. Edge Computing:

Federated learning leverages edge devices' computational capabilities, enabling real-time model training and inference directly on the devices.

Federated learning has the potential to revolutionize collaborative machine learning while addressing privacy concerns associated with centralized data collection.

20.3. Automated Machine Learning (AutoML):

Automated Machine Learning (AutoML) aims to automate various stages of the machine learning pipeline, including data preprocessing, feature selection, model selection, and hyperparameter tuning. AutoML techniques streamline the model development process and make machine learning more accessible to non-experts. Some components of AutoML include:

20.3.1. Automated Data Preprocessing:

AutoML tools automate data cleaning, handling missing values, feature scaling, and other preprocessing steps required for model training.

20.3.2. Feature Engineering:

AutoML techniques automatically generate or select relevant features from raw data, reducing the manual effort in feature engineering.

20.3.3. Hyperparameter Optimization:

AutoML tools use optimization algorithms to automatically search for the best hyperparameter values for a given model.

AutoML simplifies and accelerates the model development process, allowing data scientists to focus on higher-level tasks and problem-solving.

20.4. Deep Reinforcement Learning:

Deep reinforcement learning combines deep learning with reinforcement learning to create powerful learning systems capable of making complex decisions in dynamic environments. Deep reinforcement learning has shown remarkable success in domains like robotics, game playing, and autonomous driving. Key aspects of deep reinforcement learning include:

20.4.1. Deep Neural Networks:

Deep reinforcement learning utilizes deep neural networks as function approximators to learn policies or value functions from raw input data.

20.4.2. Markov Decision Processes:

Deep reinforcement learning algorithms learn from interactions with an environment modeled as a Markov Decision Process (MDP). They learn to take actions that maximize cumulative rewards based on observed states and rewards.

20.4.3. Exploration and Exploitation:

Deep reinforcement learning agents balance exploration (learning from new experiences) and exploitation (taking actions based on learned knowledge) to achieve optimal performance.

Deep reinforcement learning holds promise in solving complex decision-making problems that require learning from raw sensory input in dynamic environments.

Conclusion:

Data science and machine learning are continually evolving fields, driven by emerging trends and advances. Explainable AI promotes transparency and accountability in machine learning models. Federated learning enables collaborative learning while preserving data privacy. AutoML automates various stages of the machine learning pipeline, simplifying model development. Deep reinforcement learning combines deep learning and reinforcement learning to tackle complex decision-making problems. These trends are shaping the future of data science and machine learning, making them more accessible, interpretable, privacy-preserving, and capable of handling real-world challenges. By embracing these advancements, data scientists can unlock new possibilities and create impactful solutions for a wide range of applications and industries.

In this comprehensive book on data science and machine learning, we have explored a wide range of topics, techniques, and applications that form the foundation of these rapidly evolving fields. We have covered essential concepts, from data preprocessing and exploratory data analysis to advanced machine learning algorithms and deep learning architectures. Throughout the chapters, we have gained insights into the various stages of the machine learning pipeline, including data collection, feature engineering, model training, and model evaluation.

The journey began with an introduction to data science and its fundamental principles, emphasizing the importance of data quality, exploratory analysis, and data visualization. We then delved into supervised and unsupervised learning algorithms, understanding how they can be applied to solve classification, regression, clustering, and dimensionality reduction problems. We explored ensemble methods, which combine multiple models to improve predictive performance, and discussed the challenges of overfitting and model selection.

As the book progressed, we delved into specialized topics such as natural language processing, time series analysis, and recommender systems. We learned how to preprocess and analyze text data, extract meaningful features, and build models for sentiment analysis and text classification. Time series analysis introduced us to techniques for understanding and forecasting temporal data patterns, while recommender systems taught us how to generate personalized recommendations using collaborative filtering and content-based approaches.

Ethical considerations emerged as a central theme in our exploration. We discussed the importance of privacy protection, fairness, and bias mitigation in data science and machine learning. We explored techniques for addressing bias and ensuring fairness in models, as well as approaches for promoting transparency and explainability. We recognized the responsibility of data scientists in making ethical decisions and the need for frameworks that guide our actions.

Looking towards the future, we examined emerging trends and advances that are shaping the field. Explainable AI, federated learning, automated machine learning (AutoML), and deep reinforcement learning have emerged as powerful approaches that push the boundaries of data science and machine learning. These advancements aim to enhance model interpretability, protect privacy, automate workflows, and tackle complex decision-making problems.

As we conclude this book, it is evident that data science and machine learning have transformed the way we analyze data, make predictions, and solve problems. These fields continue to evolve, driven by advancements in technology, research, and the increasing availability of data. With this knowledge, readers have gained a solid foundation to embark on their own data science journeys, armed with the tools and techniques to extract valuable insights, build predictive models, and make informed decisions.

However, it is important to recognize that this book is just the beginning. Data science and machine learning are vast and ever-changing fields, and staying up-to-date with the latest research, techniques, and ethical considerations is crucial. Continuous learning, experimentation, and collaboration are essential for data scientists to adapt to new challenges and make meaningful contributions to the field.

As we move forward, let us embrace the opportunities and challenges that data science and machine learning present. Let us be responsible practitioners, considering the ethical implications of our work, striving for fairness, transparency, and accountability. Let us explore new frontiers, pushing the boundaries of what is possible, and leveraging the power of data to drive innovation and positive change.

With this book as a guide, we embark on a journey that is both exciting and humbling. Let us embark on this journey together, fostering a community of data scientists dedicated to using data science and machine learning to solve real-world problems, improve lives, and shape a better future.

Appendix: Resources and References

Stories and Lists:

"Python Mastery: Complete Python Guide from Novice to Pro" by Nibedita Sahu.

[Link: **https://nsworldinfo.medium.com/list/python-mastery-complete-python-guide-from-novice-to-pro-59845ee05372**]

"Data Science: A Comprehensive Guide" by Nibedita Sahu.

[Link: **https://nsworldinfo.medium.com/list/data-science-29618c7ebc31**]

Websites and Blogs:

Nibedita Sahu's Medium articles on Python programming and data science.

[Link: **https://nsworldinfo.medium.com/**]

Tech NS Arena YouTube channel, providing informative content and insights on various field of Technology, including data science and machine learning.

[Link: **https://youtube.com/@TechNSArena**]

Tech NS Oracle's Buy Me a Coffee page for additional resources and support.

[Link: **https://www.buymeacoffee.com/technsoracle**]

InfoWorldwithNS blog, offering articles on various tech topics, including data science.

[Link: **https://infoworldwithns.blogspot.com/**]

Research Papers:

Placeholder for relevant research papers in the field of data science and machine learning.

Note: The provided resources include the author's own articles, content, and channels. These resources offer valuable insights and knowledge to supplement the content covered in this book. Readers are encouraged to explore these resources for further learning and to stay updated with the latest developments in data science and machine learning.